THE UNIQUE BOOK OF

Songs of the Sea

vol. I

THE UNIQUE BOOK OF

Songs of the Sea
vol. I

A collection of sea chantey variations, sea songs, parodies, forecastle songs, ballads & light verse culled from newspapers around the turn of the century.

Researched and Compiled by

ROBERT E. STROM

Photography by
Mary Barker

SELF – PUBLISHED IN SALEM, MASSACHUSETTS

Table of Content

I. Sea Chantey Variations & Work Songs

II. Forecastle Songs & Ballads

III. A Pirate's Life

IV. Drinking Songs, Prohibition

V. Parodies

VI. Miscellaneous Songs

The Phoenix House

There's a speak-easy shop on Smokey Road
    Rash around, flash around!
Where the high-shouldered Screwman stand to blow
    Flash around the Phoenix House.

Six dollars it is Hoosiers' pay,
    Rash around, flash around!
We work for it both night and day,
    Flash around the Phoenix House.

Old Martin Davey wrote to me
    Rash around, flash around!
Send your boys ashore for to have a spree,
    Flash around the Phoenix House.

For every cent you make belongs to me,
    Rash around, flash around!
When they bum around this old Davey,
    Flash around the Phoenix House.

The Phoenix House in Smoky Road,
    Rash around, flash around!
When we're hard up it's there we blow,
    Flash around the Phoenix House.

New Orleans Item, June 9, 1918

Introduction

The need for clipper ships and sailing packets slowly disappeared in the mid to late nineteenth century, and the sea songs and chanteys soon followed. The sounds of the donkey engine and the steam capstan have replaced the chantey. The chantey and forecastle songs slowly moved from these vessels to the boarding houses, pubs, and along the waterfront of large seaports, keeping the tradition alive. At the turn of the century, there was a rejuvenation of interest in the history and the singing of sea chanteys and sea songs with concerts and folk music collectors. Folk music historians researched and published several song collections like *Songs of the Sea & Sailors Chanteys: An Anthology*, selected and arranged by Robert Frothingham and published in 1924, Joanna Carver Colcord's *Roll and Go, Songs of American Sailormen*, first published in 1924 and *The Making of a Sailor* written by Frederick Pease Harlow and published in Salem in 1928.

This collection includes sea chantey variations, sea songs, work songs, parodies, light verse, forecastle songs, and the occasional ballads culled over the last several years from various newspapers, libraries, and online sources. Most of these songs originated between 1850 and 1930. Several songs in this book are variations of older sea chanteys, while other songs are composed and sung in the tradition, using the voice as a vocal metronome with a pronounced rhythm. Songs like *The Dawn of a Better Cigarette* (selling *Old Gold* cigarettes) were used as advertisements, while the parody, *Billy Bone's Fancy*, is sung to the tune of the well-known chantey *Blow the Man Down*, and the song, *Cap'n Sears Kendrick* sung to the tune of *Sally Brown. Jimmy Yole's Chantey*, a humorous song, is about Yole losing his false teeth in the ocean and then finding them while dredging for quahogs.

Also included in this book is an old version of the song *Fiddler's Green* that was found in the *Springfield Republic* and dated July 1903. According to *Webster's Dictionary*, published in 1930, *Fiddler's Green* is the humorously imagined Elysian fields of sailors and craftsmen, where credit is perpetually good, and there is always a lass, a glass, and a song. The 1903 version of *Fiddler's Green* references that the tarry sailor's work on this earth is over, and as he enters *Fiddler's Green*, the sailor meets his loved ones and the sailors who went before.

Several entries include a transcription of the article leading up to the song to give the reader some background information and context. Many of these songs have no stated melody attached, giving the singer free rein to present the song choice to an old, familiar tune or make up a new melody. Several phrases were altered or omitted because of offensive language while keeping some older spellings, informal language, and slang. This collection is by no means a scholarly publication. The author intends to give the reader an interesting, enjoyable, and fun look at songs of the sea, how folks romanticized their love for the ocean, and a look at the sea music tradition at the turn of the century.

The folk music community continues to keep sea music and the sea chantey tradition and is active and vibrant with festivals, symposiums, Zoom presentations, sings, discussions, and local chantey and community gatherings.

Bob Strom

~ 1 ~

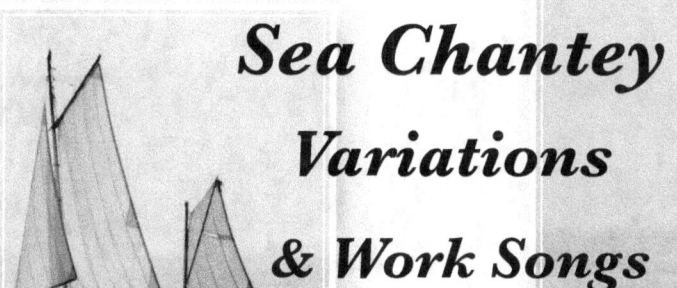

Sea Chantey

Variations

& Work Songs

The Susan Peters

The *Susan Peters* she sail from Hull,
    Heave ho, heave O Lordy.
If she ain't sunk, she's sailing still,
    Heave ho, heave O Lordy.

The *Susan Peters*, she had a crew,
    Heave ho, heave O Lordy.
And when they were aft they were forward too,
    Heave ho, heave O Lordy.

Ye see old Sue was built so quaint,
    Heave ho, heave O Lordy.
Ye could not tell the way she went,
    Heave ho, heave O Lordy.

Pawtucket Times, September 9, 1906

The Pier-Head Chantey

At the Capstan: The following chantey is literally an endless affair. In the days before donkey engines were known, heavy loads were swung inboard to the holds by means of the capstan, operated by hand and foot power. Spokes or bars being inserted into slots of the capstan-head, the men walked slowly around and around in a circle, turning the capstan by pushing against the bars. This was done while the ship was moored to the pier, and perhaps for this reason the song is called the *Pier-head Chantey*.

M.J. Powers

I've got a shipmate over yonder,
I've got a shipmate over yonder,
I've got a shipmate over yonder,
 On the yonder shore.

Bye and bye, we'll go to meet him,
Bye and bye, we'll go to meet him,
Bye and bye, we'll go to meet him,
 On the yonder shore.

For we're all going over sometime,
For we're all going over sometime,
For we're all going over sometime,
 Sit here, my darling, sometime.

Suffering time will soon be over,
Suffering time will soon be over,
Suffering time will soon be over,
 Hope I join the band.

I've got a sweetheart over yonder,
I've got a sweetheart over yonder,
I've got a sweetheart over yonder,
 On the yonder shore.

Bye and bye, I'll go to meet her,
Bye and bye, I'll go to meet her,
Bye and bye, I'll go to meet her,
   On the yonder shore.

For we're all going over sometime,
For we're all going over sometime,
For we're all going over sometime,
   Sit here, my darling, sometime.

Suffering time will soon be over,
Suffering time will soon be over,
Suffering time will soon be over,
   Hope I join the band.

New Orleans Item, June 9, 1918

Down Lima Way (fragment)

Jock's particular weakness is a song. He must know thousands of chanties, for he rolls them off like verses from the *Book of Solomon*. His voice is cracked, and his knowledge of music is probably negligible. Certainly, he betrays little evidence of any. But something for which some effort is essential, a wheezy chorus instinctively bursts from his wizened throat:

Oh, was you never down Lima way,
   Down Lima way?
There's golden rivers, so they say,
   Down Lima way.

Heave 'er taut! Heave 'er taut!
   An' clap on ev'ry stitch for Lima port,
Good-by, my bonnie lassies,
   We're off to Cal-la-o,
      Down Lima way.

He has songs for every occasion. Movement inspires him to a fresh outburst. Most of his repertoire is crudely comic, a little of it sentimental, and some quite dismally maudlin.

W. Curran Reedy, *Birmingham Herald*, July 11, 1919

Sally In Our Alley

Tune: *Bully in the Alley*

Roud No. 19807

Oh, of all the gals that sail so smart, there's none like pretty Sally,
    Raise-ho! Heave-ho! Away! Away!
For she's the darling of my heart and she lives in our alley,
    Raise-ho! Heave-ho! Away! Away!

Oh, her father he makes cabbage-necks and through the streets to cry them;
    Raise-ho! Heave-ho! Away! Away!
And her mother she sells laces long to all who please to buy them.
    Raise-ho! Heave-ho! Away! Away!

But I'm sure such folk can ne'er beget as fair a maid as Sally;
    Raise-ho! Heave-ho! Away! Away!
For she's the darling of my heart, and lives in our alley!
    Raise-ho! Heave-ho! Away! Away!

Oh, my master carry me to church; full often I am blamed, sir,
    Raise-ho! Heave-ho! Away! Away!
Because I'd leave 'em in the church, as soon as text is named, sir,
    Raise-ho! Heave-ho! Away! Away!

Oh, I leave the church at sermon time and slink away with Sally
    Raise-ho! Heave-ho! Away! Away!
For she's the darling of my heart and lives in our alley,
    Raise-ho! Heave-ho! Away! Away!

When Christmas comes about again, it's then I will have money,
    Raise-ho! Heave-ho! Away! Away!
Oh, I'll hoard it up and, box and all, I'll give it to my honey.
    Raise-ho! Heave-ho! Away! Away!

Oh, my master, and the neighbors all make game of me and Sally,
    Raise-ho! Heave-ho! Away! Away!
But it's for her I'd better be; I'd slave, and row a galley,
    Raise-ho! Heave-ho! Away! Away!

And when my seven long years are out, it's then I'd marry Sally,
    Raise-ho! Heave-ho! Away! Away!
Oh it's then we'd wed and then we'd bed, but not in Shinbone Alley,
    Raise-ho! Heave-ho! Away! Away!

New Orleans Item, June 9, 1918

Pull Down Below
Roud No. 23370

Seven long years I went to college,
    Pull down below!
Till I learned the use of artful knowledge.
    Pull down below!

Pull down, Jim Brown, my dandy fellow,
    Pull down below!
Pull down, Jim Brown, my dandy fellow.
    Pull down below!

Seven long years I courted the widder,
    Pull down below!
And seven more years I took to win her.
    Pull down below!

Pull down, Jim Brown, my dandy fellow,
    Pull down below!
Pull down, Jim Brown, my dandy fellow.
    Pull down below!

New Orleans Item, June 9, 1918

The Sailor's Song
Shenandoah

Roud No. 324

To the Editor of *The Tribune:*

Sir: I saw a letter from someone in the morning's paper, asking for the old song, *Shenandoah* – and I sent it to you as I remember it.

Pelham Manor, N.Y., Feb. 27, 1893.

Shenandoah, I love thy water;
　　Ra! ha! Oh! Rolling waters.

Shenandoah's my native valley;
　　Ra! ha! I'm going away o'er the rolling waters.

Shenandoah, I love thy daughter;
　　Ra! ha! I'm going away o'er the rolling waters.

There lives a pretty girl named Sally;
　　Ra! ha! I'm going away o'er the rolling waters.

A pretty girl, but I can't have her;
　　Ra! ha! I'm going away o'er the rolling waters.

Because I am a tarry sailor;
　　Ra! ha! I'm going away o'er the rolling waters

Seven long years, I courted Sally;
　　Ra! ha! I'm going away o'er the rolling waters.

Seven long years, but could not get her;
　　Ra! ha! I'm going away o'er the rolling waters.

I'm going away, but not forever;
　　Ra! ha! I'm going away o'er the rolling waters.

Nor let this parting friendship sever;
　　Ra! ha! I'm going away o'er the rolling waters.

New York Tribune, March 4, 1893

South Australia

Roud No. 325

In a book of far Western verse, *A Wanderer's Song of the Sea* by Charles Augustus Keeler, there is a deep-water chantey, which may remind some sailormen here about of other days:

Our barque for South Australia sails
And on a ride through trades and gales;
    Heave away, haul Away!

On South Australia I was reared,
And in the bush I grew my beard;
    Heave away, haul Away!

I love its horses and its men,
I love its wattles in the glen;
    Heave away, haul Away!

I've roamed through sun-trees' endless shade,
I've herded sheep from glade to glade;
    Heave away, haul Away!

I've mined for gold, I've played for gain,
And cruised along the Spanish main;
    Heave away, haul Away!

O South Australia's wild and free!
I had a girl, but she jilted me;
    Heave away, haul Away!

She stole my watch and ran away,
I'll meet my Kate again someday!
    Heave away, haul Away!

For we're bound for South Australia's shore
And Kate will greet me as of yore,
    Heave away, haul Away!

Boston Journal, March 29, 1903

A Capstan Chantey

Tune: *Whup Jamboree*

To the Editor of the Tribune:

Sirs: Noticing in your paper of December 4th a letter from "D.I.P." asking for some of the old-time chantey songs. I was reminded of my experience in the early 60s in the days when the *Dreadnaught* and the *Andrew Jackson*, of the *North Atlantic Line*, were leading the world in passages across the western ocean.

I am unable to give the two for which inquiry is made, *Ten Thousand Miles Away* and *The Irish Volunteers*, but I enclose a copy of one of the chanties which was very popular in the days of the *Black Ball* and *Swallow Tail* and *Tapscott lines* — a capstan chantey, sung while warping a ship into the Liverpool docks. From Memories of the 60s this sea song hails.

The chantey man sat on the capstan head and sang the song, while the men at the capstan bars, some thirty or forty of them, sang the chorus. There was always a crowd of people on the dock to hear the chantey song.

> Now, my boys be of good cheer,
>   For the Irish coast is drawing near;
> In a few days more we'll sight Cape Clear.*
>   So, Jimmy, get your oatcakes done.
>
> Chorus: Jamboree, oh, Jamboree!
>   Go away, sailor man!
>   Don't cher come nigh me!
>   Jamboree, oh, Jamboree!
>   So, Jimmy, get your oatcakes done.
>
> Now, my boys, we are all right,
>   For I think I see old Tusker Light; **
> We'll make Holyhead*** before daylight;
>   So, Jimmy, get your oatcakes done.
>
> Chorus: Jamboree, oh, Jamboree!
>   Go away, sailor man!
>   Don't cher come nigh me!
>   Jamboree, oh, Jamboree!
>   So, Jimmy, get your oatcakes done.

Now. My boys, we're round the Head,
    No more we'll eat old Tapscot's bread;
A hand in the chains to heave the lead!
    So, Jimmy, get your oatcakes done.

Chorus: Jamboree, oh, Jamboree!
        Go away, sailor man!
        Don't cher come nigh me!
        Jamboree, oh, Jamboree!
        So, Jimmy, get your oatcakes done.

And now I hear the welcome cry
    That right ahead is the old Bell Bouy;
"Keep her east-southeast!" the pilot cries.
    So, Jimmy, get your oatcakes done.

Chorus: Jamboree, oh, Jamboree!
        Go away, sailor man!
        Don't cher come nigh me!
        Jamboree, oh, Jamboree!
        So, Jimmy, get your oatcakes done.

And now, my boys, we're 'round the rock,
    Right straight into the Waterloo dock; ****
With hammocks lashed and chests all locked;
    So, Jimmy, get your oatcakes done.

Chorus: Jamboree, oh, Jamboree!
        Go away, sailor man!
        Don't cher come nigh me!
        Jamboree, oh, Jamboree!
        So, Jimmy, get your oatcakes done.

Submitted by I.O.I., to the *New York Daily Tribune*, December 12, 1913

[* Cape Clear, Ireland, ** Wexford, Ireland,
  *** Holyhead, Wales, **** Waterloo dock, Liverpool – RS]

Blow a Man Down

Roud No. 2624

The following chantey, *Blow a Man Down* is sung in two variations, in each of which the intention that is, the rhythmic accentuation of certain syllables, is distinctly its own. The first of the two versions given below is sung purely for its rhythmic effect, in setting the topsail, for instance. The second, or longer version, however, is sung at least in part with a view to making an impression on the spectators ashore, who watch the ship's crew as they toil about the capstan.

Tops'l Version

I thought I heard the old man say-ay-ay-ay;
 Gimme some time to blow a man down!
Load my ships and be away-ay-ay-ay!
 Gimme some time to blow a man down!

Capstan Version

I thought I heard the old man say
 Gimme some time to blow a man down!
Blow the man down in Mobile town!
 Gimme some time to blow a man down!

Then shake her up, my boys, and blow,
 Gimme some time to blow a man down!
In that hold the bale must go,
 Gimme some time to blow a man down!

Then shake, shake her up, my bully crew,
 Gimme some time to blow a man down!
For Irish hoosiers on the screw,
 Gimme some time to blow a man down!

You're the boys to put it through,
 Gimme some time to blow a man down!
Every lick in the fire flue,
 Gimme some time to blow a man down!

New Orleans Item, June 9, 1918

Fair Betty (fragment)

"E'll walk with sailor men no more,
    Yo, ho, an' walk the man round.

But wed a tinker an' live ashore,
    Yo, ho, an' walk the man round.

Walk the man round, walk the man round,
    Yo, ho, an' walk the man round.

For sailors is rotten as men can be,
    Yo, ho, an' walk the man round.

The bloke ashore is the bloke for me–
    Yo, ho, an' walk the man round.

Yo, ho, an' walk him round and round,
    Yo, ho, an' walk him round!"

Daily Illinois State Journal, August 13, 1922

Blow the Man Down

Roud No. 2624

Tom Gregory, Pete Kyne and Gene Overton are telling the cockeyed world what they know about sailing ships. Why, they even know the old capstan chanteys. They prove it, arms on one another's shoulders, tramping around in the old capstan circle and chanting.

As I was walking that Liverpool
    street,
(Blow the man down, bullies;
    Blow the man down!)
A beautiful maiden I chanced for
    to meet,
(Blow the man down, bullies;
    Blow the man down!)

Now tinkers and tailors and law-
    yers and all,
(Blow the man down, bullies;
    Blow the man down!)
They come to be sailors upon the
    Black Ball,
(Blow the man down, bullies;
    Blow the man down!)

Blow the man down, bullies; Blow
    the man down!
Blow the man down from Liver-
    pool town!
Rum in his guts, bullies, Bump on
    his crown,
Give us some time to Blow the
    man down.*

[* Exact transcription from newspaper — RS]

New Orleans States, December 8, 1929

The Banks of the Sacramento

Roud No. 319

Thus the heavy sails are set, and lighter ones follow; the towline is cast off; England's white cliffs fade away astern as the sun sinks below the horizon ahead; night comes down, with its vague fear for the new voyager's heart, its commonplaceness to the ocean's wanderers, and we are alone to do our business on the waters. Now days slip by on the heels of night; night goes as uneventfully after it; they stretch into weeks; the breeze freshens, and we tauten halyards to the somewhat lively tune of *The Banks of the Sacramento*, the first part being:

> Now, my lads, get your beds and lie down,
>> With a hoo-dah! (All pull together.)
> Now, my lads, get your beds and lie down,
>> With a hoo-dah, hoo-dah-o! (Pull.)
>
> Blow, boys, blow for Californio,
>> With a hoo-dah!
> There's plenty of gold, so I've been told,
> On the Banks of the Sacramento.
>> With a hoo-dah, hoo-dah-o!
>
> We came to the river where we couldn't get across,
>> With a hoo-dah!
> And the plenty of gold, as you'll now be told,
> Was a bully, bully, bully loss.
>> With a hoo-dah, hoo-dah-o!

J.E. Patterson, *New York Daily Tribune*, September 9, 1900

The Dutchman

The following is an example of a "fly-time" chantey, which were generally sung without particular motive, but which could be converted, upon occasion, into working chanteys:

> Oh, they put me in the calaboose
>   For knocking a Dutchman down.
> And I thought they'd never turn me loose
>   For knocking a Dutchman down.
>
> Oh, it's roll me over, Judy dear,
>   For knocking a Dutchman down.
> And I'll go with you when I get clear
>   For knocking a Dutchman down.
>
> If you come with me, when I do go
>   For knocking a Dutchman down.
> I'll take you where calm winds do blow
>   For knocking a Dutchman down.
>
> She says, "I will take you to Sailor's Hall
>   For knocking a Dutchman down.
> And introduce you to the ladies all"
>   For knocking a Dutchman down.
>
> "And I'm sure they will hug you, one and all
>   For knocking a Dutchman down.
> And we'll drink to the health of old *Black Ball*"
>   For knocking a Dutchman down.
>
> "We'll all go down to Jack Story's bar
>   For knocking a Dutchman down.
> And we'll drink to the health of the old *Black Star*"
>   For knocking a Dutchman down.

New Orleans Item, June 9, 1918

Chain Gang Chantey

"They originated in the south and while never written, due to occasional obscenity, are well known by most of the prisoners, railroad workers and hobos," he explained in polished phrases.

One mournful chantey, in which you can almost hear the thud of chain gang pickaxes, goes:

> Every mail day,
>   Mail day I get a letter,
> Cryin' son come home,
>   Lord, Lord, my son come home.
>
> I never had no—
>   Never had no ready made money;
> I couldn't go home,
>   Lord, Lord, I couldn't go home.
>
> I'm gonna roll here,
>   Roll here a few days longer;
> And then go home,
>   Lord, Lord, and then go home.
>
> If I can make it,
>   June, July, and August;
> I'll be a man,
>   Lord, Lord, I'll be a man.
>
> But look up yonder,
>   Hot boilin' sun is turnin' over;
> It won't go down,
>   Lord, Lord, It won't go down.

Cleveland Plain Dealer, January 20, 1935

Corn-Shucking Song

The lightwood fire was made near the corn house, and the [blacks] dropped in from the neighboring plantation, singing as they came. The driver of the plantation, a colored man, brought out baskets of corn in the husk, and piled it in a heap; and the [blacks] began to strip the husks from the ears, singing with great glee as they worked, keeping time to the music, and now and then throwing in a joke and an extravagant burst of laughter, The songs were generally of a comic character; but one of them was set to a singularly wild and plaintive air, which some of our musicians would do well to reduce to notation. These are the words:

>Johnny come down de hollow.
>>Oh hollow!
>Johnny come down de hollow.
>>Oh hollow! *
>Boys, go catch me pony.
>>Oh hollow!
>Bring him 'round de corner.
>>Oh hollow!
>I'm goin' away to Georgia.
>>Oh hollow!
>Boys, good-bye forever!
>>Oh hollow!

>>W.C. Bryant, Esq., senior editor of the *New York Evening Post,*
>>*Salem Register,* May 1, 1843

[* Three verses were left off — RS]

Haul Away Rosy (fragment)

Roud No. 809

Street Songs of Charleston Hucksters: They congregate there to receive the boatloads of fresh "vegetables." Long before even these enterprising citizens of the sleepy town are up and doing, the "Mosquito fleet" has put to sea while the still, gray dawn is breaking, and you hear them sending back in calm weather the long, faint cadence of a rowing song:

> Rosy am a handsome gal!
> Haul away Rosy— Haul away gal!
>
> Fancy Slippers and fancy shawl!
> Haul away Rosy— Haul away gal!
>
> Rosy going to the fancy ball!
> Haul away Rosy— Haul away gal!

Even in wet and windy weather, when the wind is fresh, and strong, sails are hoisted, and silently the fleet flits out like a flock of ghostly birds across the harbor, across the bar and out to the banks, forty miles away.

All of the folk songs have a queer minor catch in them, and even the street cries have an echo of sadness in their closing cadence.

From the *Christian Science Monitor,* reprinted in *Iowa Evening Nonpareil,* June 17, 1920

Chantey of the River (fragment)

Flatboats of the Ohio were to the Middle West what the 'iron horse' was to the far west after the Civil War. As they float down the river the Pilgrims of the Ohio sing:

> O, the river is up, the channel is deep,
> The wind blows steady and strong,
> A splashing their oars the mariners keep
> As they row their boats along.
>
> Chorus: Down the river,
> Down the river,
> Down the O-Hi-O.

Omaha Monitor, June 18, 1926

The Natchez

Old Time Songs of the Roustabouts and Deck Hands.

No one who has ever heard the wild yet melodious songs of a black steamboat crew, away down the Mississippi River while "wooding up," can forget it. The boat has landed at some quiet, uninhabitable looking sort of a place and lays lazily alongside the full banks, while the overhanging cypress, with its long and graceful festoons of moss touch the hurricane deck. The passengers are out on the shore-side guards watching the men file in with their monstrous loads of cordwood, and out again empty-handed, singing their peculiar songs all the time. The forest is lit up with the flaming torches, and the quaint refrain of dusky minstrels as they move in the uncertain light makes up a weird scene. In these songs, as in everything else, human there is a leader. He gives out anything that occurs to him, in a sort of strange solo, and the others come in on the chorus. The favorite sort of a song is in words something like this:

> The Natchez is a bully boat,
> > Hi-oh-oh,
> She walks on the water,
> > Hi-oh-oh,
> The Captain he's a clever man,
> > Hi-oh-oh,
> And his mate is here from Georgia,
> > Hi-oh-oh,

Harrisburg Patriot, March 6, 1875

Leave Her, Johnny, Leave Her

Roud No. 354

The times were hard and the wages low,
    Leave Her, Johnny, Leave Her,
The times were hard and the wages low,
    And now it's time to, Leave Her.

Since the day we sailed from Birkenhead
    Leave Her, Johnny, Leave Her,
They whacked us out of a pound of bread;
    And now it's time to, Leave Her.

Our work was hard and the voyage was long,
    Leave Her, Johnny, Leave Her,
The seas were high and the gales were strong,
    And now it's time to, Leave Her.

The food was bad and the wages low,
    Leave Her, Johnny, Leave Her,
But now on shore again we'll go;
    And now it's time to, Leave Her.

The sails are furled and our work is done,
    Leave Her, Johnny, Leave Her,
And now on shore we'll have some fun,
    And now it's time to, Leave Her.

~ 2 ~

Forecastle Songs
& Ballads

Off to Sea Once More

Roud No. 644

I met with a gay young 'Frisco gal,
　　And my heart was not my own,
But when I kissed her goodbye at last,
　　My money and watch was gone.
As I was walking down the street,
　　And people was gazing at me,
Said they, "There's a brave young sailor lad,
　　Who's off once more to sea."

Chorus: Once more, once more,
　　　　　He's off to sea once more,
　　　　Oh, there's a brave young sailor lad,
　　　　Who's off to sea once more.

A boarding master picked me up,
　　His name was Shanghai Brown,
And I'll tell you the truth, he wasn't so ill,
　　For he gave me half a crown,
"Look here, my brave young sailor lad,
　　There's no more work ashore,
But here's your chance, take ten pounds advance
　　And go to sea once more.

Chorus: Once more, once more,
　　　　　He's off to sea once more,
　　　　Oh, there's a brave young sailor lad,
　　　　Who's off to sea once more.

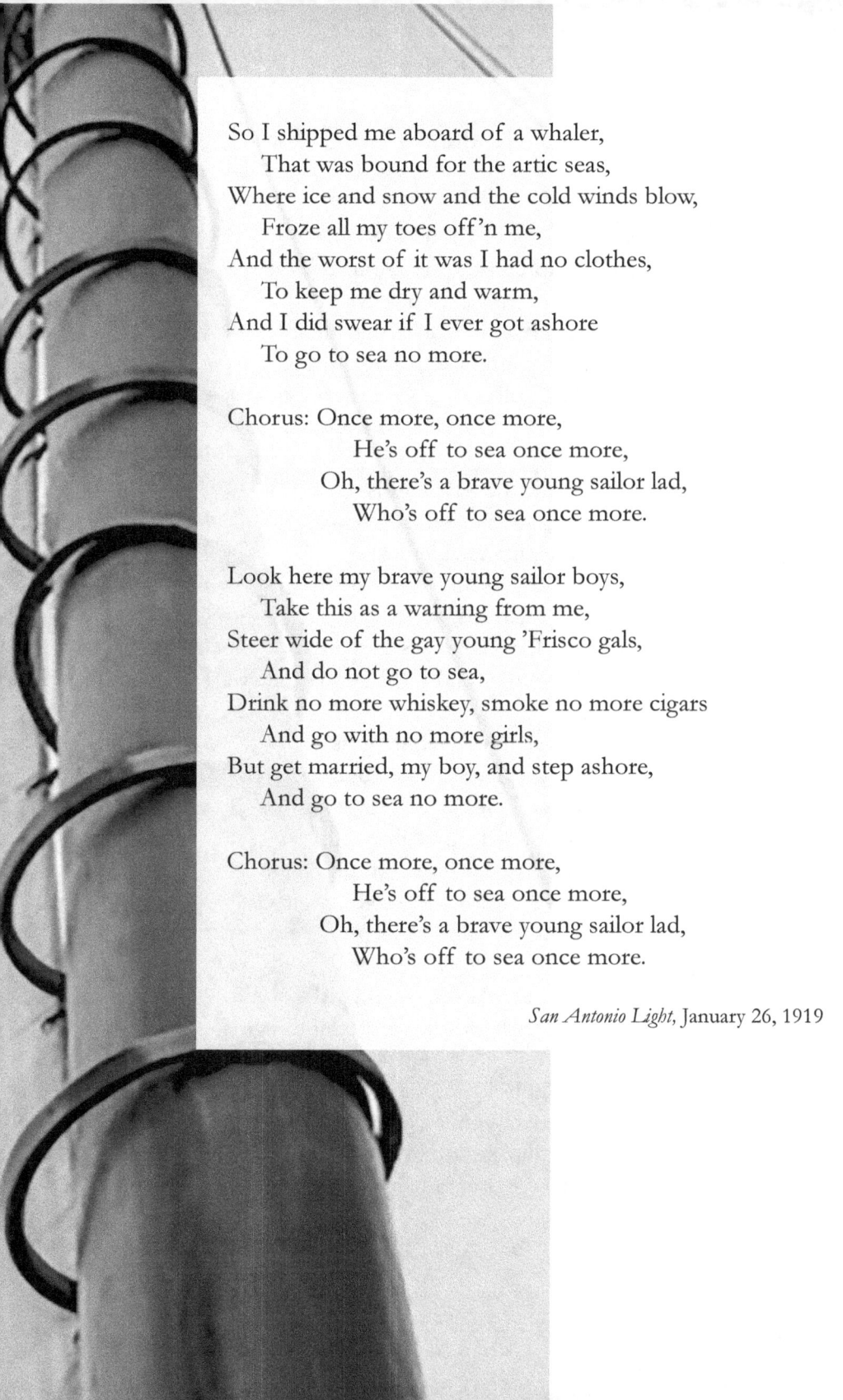

So I shipped me aboard of a whaler,
　　That was bound for the artic seas,
Where ice and snow and the cold winds blow,
　　Froze all my toes off'n me,
And the worst of it was I had no clothes,
　　To keep me dry and warm,
And I did swear if I ever got ashore
　　To go to sea no more.

Chorus: Once more, once more,
　　　　He's off to sea once more,
　　　　Oh, there's a brave young sailor lad,
　　　　Who's off to sea once more.

Look here my brave young sailor boys,
　　Take this as a warning from me,
Steer wide of the gay young 'Frisco gals,
　　And do not go to sea,
Drink no more whiskey, smoke no more cigars
　　And go with no more girls,
But get married, my boy, and step ashore,
　　And go to sea no more.

Chorus: Once more, once more,
　　　　He's off to sea once more,
　　　　Oh, there's a brave young sailor lad,
　　　　Who's off to sea once more.

San Antonio Light, January 26, 1919

What Pleases The Girls

What'll please the Gloucester girls,
The Gloucester girls, the Gloucester girls -
    What'll please 'em, say?
    Fiddle and dance the whole night long,
    Sit at the window and sing a song;
That's what'll please the Gloucester girls;
        They're bound to be lively, anyway!

What'll please the Salem girls,
The Salem girls, the Salem girls -
    What'll please 'em, say?
    Laces and fans and silks and shawls,
    Drinking tea and paying calls;
That's what'll please the Salem girls;
        They're bound to be genteel, anyway!

What'll please the Newbury girls,
The Newbury girls, the Newbury girls -
    What'll please 'em, say?
    John speed with four-in-hand;
    Chowder parties down on the sand;
That's what'll please the Newbury girls;
        They're bound to be going, anyway!

What'll please the Portsmouth girls,
The Portsmouth girls, the Portsmouth girls -
    What'll please 'em, say?
    A Captain bold and devil-may-care;
    Or any man with a taking air;
That's what'll please the Portsmouth girls;
        They're bound to be married, anyway!

Found by Beth and Jeff Welin, Manchester Historical Society,
Salem Gazette, mid 1850s

Windlass Song

Heave at the windlass!– Heave O, Cheerily, Men!
Heave all at once, with a will;
The tide's quickly making,
Our cordage a-creaking,
The water has put on a frill,
Heave O!

Fare-you-well, sweetheart!– Heave O, Cheerily, Men!
Shore gambarado and sport!
The good ship all ready,
The dog-vane all steady,
The wind blowing dead out of port,
Heave O!

Once in blue water!– Heave O, Cheerily, Men!
Blow it from north or from south,
She'll stand to it brightly,
And curtsey politely,
And carry a bone in her mouth,
Heave O!

Short cruise or long cruise– Heave O, Cheerily, Men!
Jolly Jack Tar thinks it one.
No latitude dreads he,
Of White, Black, or Red Sea;
Great icebergs, or tropical sun;
Heave O!

One other turn, and Heave O, Cheerily, Men!
Heave, and good-bye to the shore;
Our money, how went it?
We shared it and spent;
Next year we'll come back with some more.
Heave O!

Salem Register, October 24, 1853

Fiddler's Green

At a place called *Fiddler's Green*, there do all honest mariners take their pleasure after death. And there are Admirals with their dear Ladies, and fearless Adventures with the Sweethearts of their youth, and tarry handed Sailormen laughing in cottage gardens.

Never again shall we beat out to sea,
    In driven mist, and sleet like bitter tears,
To watch the harbor beacons fade, a lee,
    And people all the sea-room with our fears.

All toil is done! No more, no more do we,
Square the slow yards, and stagger on the sea.

No more the weariness of day and day
    Unchanged, unshadowed, where the weed drifts by,
And leaden fish pass rolling at their play,
    And changeless suns crawl up an empty sky.

Our watch is done! No more, no more do we
Pray for the wind to break the polished sea.

Cities we saw, white wall and glinting dome,
    And palm-fringed islands dreaming on the blue,
To us, more fair the rugged cliffs of home,
    The climbing roofs, the laughter ringing true.

The voyage is done! No more, no more do we
Scan the strange lamps along the stranger quay.

Night comes! To each the night that he loves best,
    In some dear garden where the roses sleep,
And no quick clouds bank up along the West,
    There is no sail to furl, no watch to keep.

Now all is done! No more, no more do we
Shout our rude chanties, toiling on the sea.

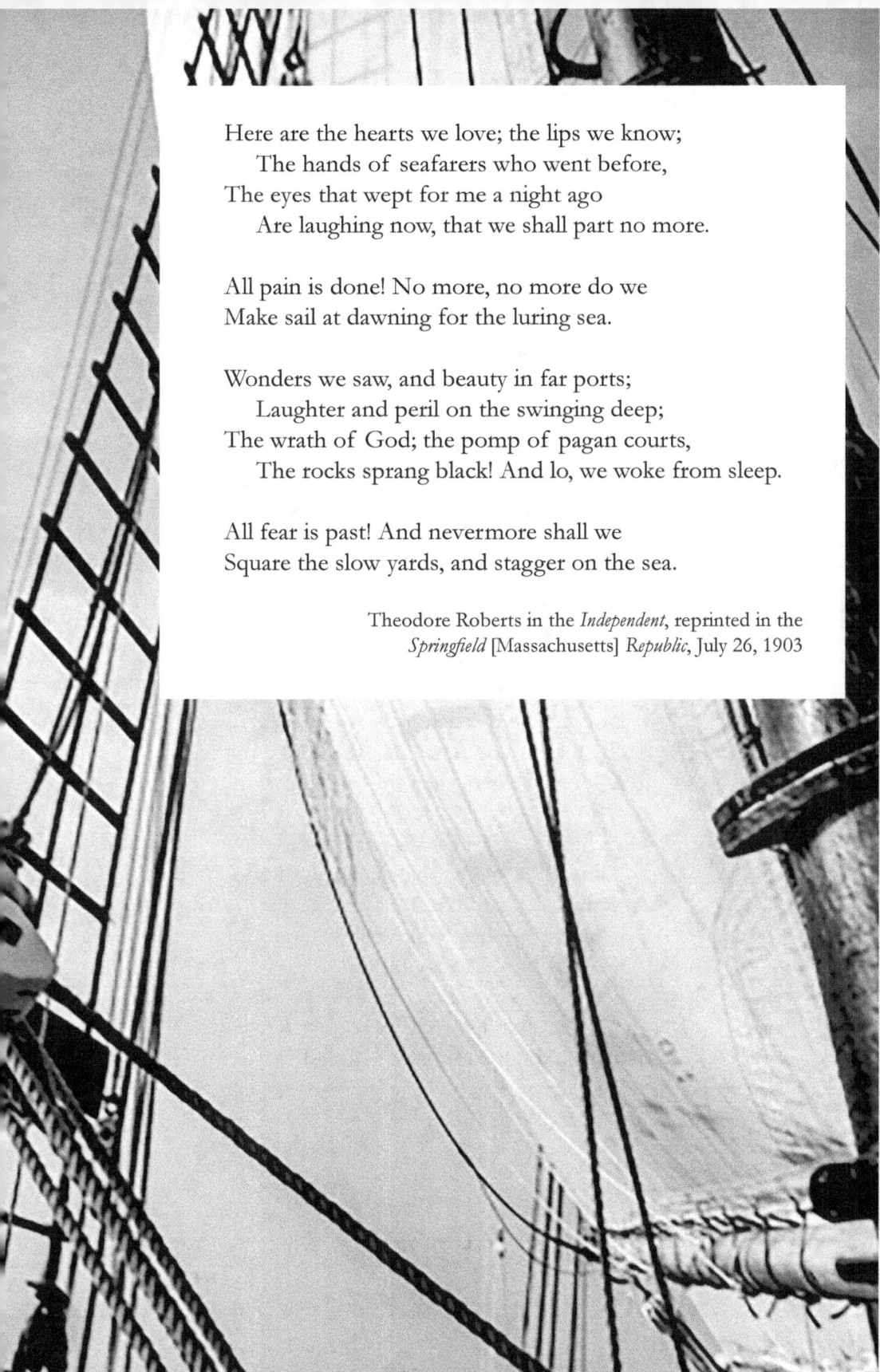

Here are the hearts we love; the lips we know;
    The hands of seafarers who went before,
The eyes that wept for me a night ago
    Are laughing now, that we shall part no more.

All pain is done! No more, no more do we
Make sail at dawning for the luring sea.

Wonders we saw, and beauty in far ports;
    Laughter and peril on the swinging deep;
The wrath of God; the pomp of pagan courts,
    The rocks sprang black! And lo, we woke from sleep.

All fear is past! And nevermore shall we
Square the slow yards, and stagger on the sea.

Theodore Roberts in the *Independent*, reprinted in the
Springfield [Massachusetts] *Republic*, July 26, 1903

The Homeward Bound

Tune: *Ten Thousand Miles Away*

Roud No. 927

Oh, for a brisk and fresh'ning wind
    That follows the tall ship fast,
That curls the crests of the sun kiss'd seas,
    And strains the pitch pine mast,
    And bends the towering mast,
Whilst the dog-watch yarns go 'round,
    And the chanteyman uplifts his voice,
In the song of the homeward bound!

The chorus ascends, in time and tune,
    And is caught on the rising wind,
Till the startled gulls with fluttering wing
    Fall off in the track behind,
    Fall off in the flakes behind,
Where their shrieks and screams are drowned,
    By the proud, long song, the loud, proud song,
The song of the homeward bound.

Give me the midst of a stormy zone,
    Where the staggering sun swings low,
And the clouds roll back on the weatherboard,
    Predicting a heavy blow,
    Sure sign of a heavy blow,
When from windward comes the sound,
    Of the thunder's roar to rouse the song,
The song of the homeward bound.

Give me the man with the rich, round voice,
  When the wind is bellowing hard,
As he looms his reach o'er the leading block,
  A-hoisting a topsail yard,
  Mast heading a topsail yard,
As the sail sets taut and round,
  And the word "Belay!" falls like "Amen"
To the song of the homeward bound.

Oh! The strange seafolk, the wild seafolk,
  That live on the trackless deep,
That carry our commerce the world around,
  Where ever the wild waves ever sweep!
  Where the wild waves sweep,
To these let the toast resound
  With a health to the sailor, a health to the ship,
And a health to the homeward bound!

T.H. Mathias, From the *San Francisco Seamen's Journal*,
Cleveland Plain Dealer, June 11, 1899

The Derby (Darby) Ram
Roud No. 126

A few months since, a letter was published in the *Springfield* [Mass.] *Republican* giving an account of an invitation from Chief-Justice Oliver Ellsworth, to Gen. [George] Washington, then in Hartford, to dine with him at his residence in Windsor; and which was sent and delivered by Judge Ellsworth's son Martin, then a lad, with much fear and trembling. Interest is also renewed in this visit by the exhibition at your late Washington tea party of several articles used on that occasion. During the visit, Gen. Washington appeared in a novel and interesting scene. Entering the nursery, where were two twin boys, two years old (afterward the late Gov. Ellsworth and the Hon. Henry L. Ellsworth), he took one on each knee and sang to them this song, often repeated in after years by the governor with much zest.

> As I was going to Derby,
>   Upon a market day,
> I spied the biggest ram, sir,
>   That ever was fed on hay.
>   Tow de row de row,
>   Tow de row de da.
>
> He had four feet to walk, sir,
>   He had four feet to stand,
> And every foot he had, sir,
>   Covered an acre of land.
>   Tow de row de row,
>   Tow de row de da.
>
> The wool upon his back, sir,
>   It reaches to the sky,
> And eagles build their nests there,
>   For I heard their young ones cry.
>   Tow de row de row,
>   Tow de row de da.
>
> The wool upon his tail, sir,
>   I heard the weaver say,
> Made three thousand yards of cloth,
>   For he wove it all in a day.
>   Tow de row de row,
>   Tow de row de da.

The butcher that cut his throat, sir,
  Was drowned in the blood,
And the little boy who held the bowl,
  Was carried away in the flood.
    Tow de row de row,
      Tow de row de da.

Boston Christian Register, May 13, 1876

John Brown's Body (fragment)

John Brown's body lies a-moldering in a grave,
  John Brown's body lies a-moldering in a grave,
John Brown's body lies a-moldering in a grave,
  As we go rolling home!

And it's glory, glory, hallelujah!
  And it's glory, glory, hallelujah!
And it's glory, glory, hallelujah!
  As we go rolling home!

Washington D.C., *Evening Star,* August 8, 1924

Your Song

There's a lay that's sung by the roving man,
  There's a chantey that lifts from the sea,
There's a coral that blows from the northern snow—
  And the song you sing to me.

You sing of love in a little home,
  'Tis the song I like the best,
For you and home, where'er I roam,
  Mean comfort and peace and rest.

Clifford Reynolds Knights, *Trenton Evening Times,* May 9, 1920

Forecastle Rhymery

Air: *Auld Lang Syne*

The following stanzas were handed us by a young sailor from the Pacific, a foremast hand on board ship, *Maria* of this port, who assured us they are bona fide his own production, composed and penned on board ship, just as the last voyage was up, and the ship's prow turned homewards. If they bespeak no extraordinary poetical genius, the lines, in the chirographic dress worn by the manuscript, indicate at least a steady hand.

At last that joyful day has come
    We've long in fancy view'd –
The appointed tour, from sea to sea,
    Our voyage we have pursued.

Three years we've toiled upon the waves
    And ranged the Ocean through,
'Midst storms and tempests we have sailed,
    A gay and gallant crew.

We've stemmed the broad Pacific tides,
    Through gloomy scenes and gay;
But now to each will bid farewell,
    And here no longer stay.

Our gallant ship is gathering way
    Before the rising breeze,
To hear us to our distant home,
    Far o'er the stormy seas.

Come all who roam these distant climes,
    Give us a parting cheer,
We're bound unto our native land,
    That home to all so dear.

Ye powers propitious on us smile,
　　As we our way explore
Towards our friends and happy homes,
　　On fair New England's shore.

While sailing on the raging main,
　　Bound for our native shore,
We'll sing our song, and tell our tales,
　　Of toils and trials o'er.

When gathering storms around us lower,
　　And our onward course oppose,
Each anxious mind will dream of home
　　Forgetting present woes.

And when that welcome coast we view,
　　We'll greet th' auspicious day,
And with united voices shout,
　　Hail! Fair Columbia!

At last when we've moor'd our ship
　　Safe in our destined port,
We'll dwell no more on dangers past
　　But join each merry sport.

Once more we'll greet our early friends,
　　The ancient and the gay,
And in the social circle all,
　　We'll spend each happy day.

Again through lovely vales we'll roam,
　　Inhale the balmy breeze,
And 'mid the bowers of love again
　　We'll saunter at our ease.

R.M. Dix—n, *Nantucket Inquirer,* March 26, 1836

A Whaling We'll All Go

Of Whalers, too, we bring long lists so fine,
 Of lucky voyages, their course and plan,
Who fly beneath the fervour of the time,
 Or freeze their knuckles somewhere off Japan;

Merry as grigs the while – hearty and strong, trolling some ditty like the following:

 Come all ye sturdy sailors,
  And hearken unto me,
I'll sing about the whalers
  That traverse yonder sea;
  And a whaling we'll all go, we'll go, we'll go,
   And a whaling we'll all go.

 'Tis always our vocation
  To face the mighty foe,
We benefit the nation
  And help ourselves also,
  When a whaling we do go, do go, do go,
   Then a whaling we'll all go.

 We leave it all for other
  To war for human spoil,
For we're a band of brothers
  That rather have sperm oil,
  When a whaling we do go, do go, do go,
   When a whaling we all go.

 And when we catch Leviathan
  We stick him with a spade,
And haul his jacket higher than
  Old Tommy Never's* head,
  While a whaling we all go, awe go, we go,
   And a whaling we all go.

We mince him into pieces,
    Let winds blow East or West;
And when stripped off his fleece is,
    The goneys take the rest,
      While a whaling we all go, we go, we go,
      And a whaling we all go.

And when our good ship's tonnage
    Is all completely stored,
We stow away the dunnage,
    Get home, and safely moored,
      For a whaling we all go, we go , we go,
      And a whaling we'll all go.

The push about the jorum,
    Let's take a social glass,
Preserving due decorum
    While drinking to each lass,
      And a whaling we all go, we'll go , we'll go,
      Then a whaling we'll all go.

And now I'll give a great hint
    Concerning all this whale,–
If you don't find much weight in't
    Why take it then by tale,
      And a whaling still I'll go, and go, and go,
      And a whaling we'll all go.

Nantucket Inquirer, January 6, 1827

[* Tom Never, a member of the Nantucket Wampanoag Never family.
According to tradition, Tom Never kept watch for whales from a station
on the high point on Nantucket's southeast corner that bears his name.
Nantucket Historical Association – RS]

The Dreadnought's Song (fragment)
Roud No. 924

Will Captain Clark pay $100 for the Evidence of a Sea Chantey?

To the Editor of the *Sun* – Sir: My attention has been called to an article in the *Sun* entitled "The Evidence Against the Ship *Dreadnought's* Record."

In the article, there is not one word about the record made by the *Dreadnought's* famous rival, the *Jeremiah Thompson*. There were many shipping merchants and old salts in those days who claimed that the clipper ship *Jeremiah Thompson* made a better record.

There are two ways for Captain Clark or your correspondent to get on the trail of the true record of that famous trip of the *Dreadnought*. Let them go down to the Sailor's Snug Harbor on Staten Island, and if any of the old salts of fifty years ago are still anchors there, recite these two verses to them:

> She is a packet,
> A packet of fame,
> She hails from New York,
> And the Dreadnought's her name;
> She sails o'er the Atlantic,
> Where the stormy winds blow,
> She's a rip roaring clipper,
> Oh, boys, watch her go.

> Now we are sailing
> Off the Long Island shore,
> The pilot just left us,
> As he oft done before;
> Good-bye to New York
> And the girls we adore,
> We're off for Liverpool
> In the Dreadnought once more.

If there are any old timers listening, let Captain Clark or your correspondent say to them: "Boys, there's a hole in the ballad, and if any of you will recite or sing to me the remaining nine or ten verses of the *Dreadnought*, I will pay you $100 for your trouble."

But if any of the old salts are still in the Snug Harbor these verses, not the money, will awaken memories.

If Captain Clark or your correspondent meet with no success at the Harbor let him place an advertisement in the Baltimore papers offering a reward to any person having a copy of the song entitled, *The Dreadnought*.

A truthful log of the record trip will be found in that song. I will explain why I know.

In 1859 and for forty years afterward my folks kept a sailor's boarding house in New York. Among our boarders was one called the Rhymer, who was on the *Dreadnought* when she made that record trip. He was noted for writing in rhymes the description of the voyages he made and also a log for each day's run.

There was a difference of several hours between Captain Samuel's log and the Rhymer's log. The Rhymer's song was made up of about twelve verses; the majority of them referring to the distance the *Dreadnought* sailed each day on her famous trip. I am no sailor; that is why the remaining verses of the Rhymer's log did not remain in my memory.

Billy Smiles, New Haven, Conn. May 28.

Billy Smiles, *Sun and New York Press*, May 30, 1917

The Screwmen

In eighteen hundred and sixty-five
    When screwmen's wages were four and five,
We come to the conclusion, one fine day,
    That six and seven was Mobile pay.

    So hand and heart went every man,
        And quit each ship did every gang,
    And swore they'd live on musty beans
        Before they'd work for less in New Orleans.

But Captain Russell, the old sot,
    Said he'd lay up the *Vanguard* until she'd rot,
Before for working nine hours a day,
    He'd pay six and seven screwmen's pay.

    It's just two weeks them Screwmen stood,
        Until their wages was made good,
    And then old Russell, the dammed old swine,
        See that he had to come to time.

Straightway he went unto McNeil,
    Said: "Sandy, my lad, I've got a sail,
I see those fellows can't be fooled,
    So you'd better put your tools aboard!"

    Says McNeil: "They're men all of one mind,
        Such men as them it's hard to find,
    And if they ask you for ten dollars a day,
        You might as well pay it and have no more to say.

Before that they'd work under pay
    On your own soup bones ye'd have to lay,
If you wanted to get the *Van* afloat,
    You'd pay them the wages, I'd take my oath."

Now we've got our wages to a man,
　　Like men we'll work in every gang,
And when our pockets they get flush,
　　We'll spend it on hot whiskey punch.

New Orleans Item, September 9, 1918

Row Well Ye Mariners

The tide is for the shore, boys,
　　And gently blows a fav'ring wind,
We'll soon touch land once more, boys,
　　And leave the billowy ways behind.

　　Row steady and strong,
　　　　The way it is long,
　　So bend to your oars,
　　　　And join in our song.

　　　　Row well, Row well,
　　　　Row well ye Mariners.

A welcome voice is hailing,
　　Give answer mates with a hearty cheer,
Our sturdy strokes prevailing,
　　Full soon the harbour will appear.

　　Then speed her with skill,
　　　　The waters are still,
　　Our strokes are directed
　　　　With right good will.

　　　　Row well, Row well,
　　　　Row well ye Mariners.

English Melodies from the 13th to the 18th Centuries, J.M. Dent & Sons,
Quincy Patriot Ledger, December 20, 1928

The Long Chantey

A Soothing Chantey: There were the songs, which were chanted during rough weather to inspire sea-sick passengers with the idea that everything was all right. Of course, there are no set verses. If the known verses came to an end, and there was need for more singing, additional words were improvised for the occasion.

Oh, I shipped aboard a packet, strange countries to go see,
    Ho-Ho, Haya-haya-hee-yip!
And it's there I fell in tow with a pretty Judy gal,
    Good morning, ladies, all around.

Oh, I had a little money, and I thought I'd have a spell,
    Ho-Ho, Haya-haya-hee-yip!
And I spent all my money, along with that Irish gal,
    Good morning, ladies, all around.

When the money it was done, I thought she'd turn me away,
    Ho-Ho, Haya-haya-hee-yip!
But she says to me: "Young sailor lad, it's here you've got to stay!"
    Good morning, ladies, all around.

Oh, it's now I've married that Irish gal, I'll go to sea no more,
    Ho-Ho, Haya-haya-hee-yip!
And for to support that Irish gal, I'm bound to stay ashore,
    Good morning, ladies, all around.

So I come down on that *Natchez*, and I went upon the *Lee*,
    Ho-Ho, Haya-haya-hee-yip!
And the way they wooded Mickey up, I'm sure you'd pity me,
    Good morning, ladies, all around.

There was the captain on the boiler deck, a-scratching of his head,
    Ho-Ho, Haya-haya-hee-yip!
A-swearing at the old dockhand, a-heaving of the load.
    Good morning, ladies, all around.

"If you can't lead the boat no better, just throw away the line,"
    Ho-Ho, Haya-haya-hee-yip!
Just then the deckie he sung out, "A quarter less twain."
    Good morning, ladies, all around.

So it's now I'm safely married, I'll go steam-boating no more,
    Ho-Ho, Haya-haya-hee-yip!
For to support my Irish wife, I'm bound to stay ashore.
    Good morning, ladies, all around.

For to support my Irish wife, I'm bound to stay ashore,
    Ho-Ho, Haya-haya-hee-yip!
And I'll work upon the levee with a master stevedore.
    Good morning, ladies, all around. *

New Orleans Item, June 9, 1918

[* Verses 1 and 8 were omitted because of language – RS]

Sweep Over a Sailor's Grave

The Seamen's Widow and Orphan Association make their annual appeal to the public, for sympathy and aid in their benevolent operations, on Sunday evening next. They have never yet called upon our community in vain; and God forbid that they ever shall while we have a merchant to plan a voyage, a sailor to go down to the sea in ships, or a human heart among us to yearn after a loved one that roams over the mighty waters. But there are special reasons why, at this time, their appeal should be met with more whole-souled and generous response than ever. The perils to which the mariner is exposed have been brought home to us all more closely and vividly than ever before. The howlings of the tempests, which have shattered so many fair barks and swept whole crews away in an instant, are yet ringing in our ears. The records of disaster, suffering, and death are appallingly long and sad, and their end is not yet. Widows and orphans, in rapidly increased numbers, need our aid. Their cup of sorrow is full; their hearts are crushed; their homes are desolate; their means of living are scanty and inadequate to the exigencies of this most inclement winter and the unusually high prices of all the necessaries of life. And they are sailors' wives and children – loved ones of the fearless, frank, generous sons of ocean, to whom distress never appeals in vain and whose hands are never closed over the purse strings when messmates, friends, or stranger needs relief.

There is within the lone, lone sea
A spot unmarked, but holy,
For there the gallant and the free,
In his ocean bed lies lowly;
In his ocean bed lies lowly;

Down, down beneath the deep
That oft in triumph bore him,
He sleeps a sound and peaceful sleep,
With the salt waves dashing o'er him.
With the salt waves dashing o'er him.

He sleeps, he sleeps serene and safe,
From tempest and from billow,
Where storms that high above his chase,
Scarce rock his peaceful pillow.
Scarce rock his peaceful pillow.

The sea and him, in death,
They did not dare to sever,
It was his home when he had breath,
'T is now his home forever.
'T is now his home forever.

Surely, in this community, which has been so much indebted to the sailor from the beginning of its history to this day, the utmost demand, which can be made upon its active sympathies, will be fully and cheerfully met. We have no doubt about it. There is hardly a navigable sea that has not been visited by Salem Ships. There is scarcely a port in the wide world that has not echoed to the manly voices of Salem crews. There is no pestilence, no disease in foreign lands, no form of accident, no peril of the sea, no danger from savage islander or cruel idolater, that the Salem sailor has not encountered, and of which he has not been the victim. There is scarcely a family among us that has not some relative, or friend, or acquaintance among the seamen. The ocean, the great highway of nations flows to our very doors. We look out upon its restless heaving from our windows. Often, in the stillness of night, we pause and listen to the solemn, subdued roar of its wild surgings against our rockbound coast; and, when the tempest rages, as we gather around the hearthstone, secure in our homes, "God help the mariner!" is the impulsive prayer that gushes out from every heart.

Ah, the wintry storms, how effectively they appeal to us on behalf of the sailor's widow and orphan! They strew our coast with wrecks; they wail the requiem of the last mariner; they sweep over the sailor's grave. Alas! How many of us can say, with hearts yet tenderly alive to the sorrow of bereavement.

Henry Francis Lyte, *Salem Register,* February 9, 1854

The Chantey of Cap'n Foster

To the Editor of the Boston Herald:

This chantey, symbolical of modern days and modern ways, was sent to me last summer from Paris, to cheer me up during a tedious convalescence in the hospital, when recovering from a major operation. I do not know the author but it seems to rollicking to let die on my desk.   E.L.S.

Now list ye well and to a tale I'll tell you
    Of Capt'n Phineas Foster,
Who sailed the sea in the *Nancy Lee,*
    A ship from the port of Gloucester
Of Pilgrim stock, and Plymouth Rock,
    A devout man was the Capt'n.
Who never swore, afloat or ashore,
    Nor drank, whate'er might happen,

He loved a doll by the name of Moll,
    A Milliner up in Salem.
An ancient town, of great renown
    Where witches, once they'd jail 'em.
He pressed his suit, to win this beaut,
    Who was titled Mollie Kidder.
But she turned him down, with a frigid frown,
    This flirty and fickle widder.

Chorus: Oh, blow, ye wild winds, blow,
            Reef sail with a couple of hitches,
        She gave him the air,
        With a haughty stare,
            For he had no worldly riches.

She told Capt'n Phin he would never win,
    For a millionaire she'd marry,
Or she'd stay unwed till she went plumb dead,
    For she was a gold-diggin' fairy.

The Cap. in pain, went most insane,
    And he figgered and he figgered,
But he didn't know where to get the dough,
    Be keel-hauled and be jiggered.

His first mate said, "Cap use your head.
    Why should you go a-beggin?
Just take your ship, on a southern trip
    And do some fast bootlegging."
So, they put to sea in the *Nancy Lee*,
    And the Puritanical Foster.
Put the law at naught, because he thought,
    That widder he had lost her.

Chorus: So, blow, ye wild winds, blow,
          There's plenty of liquor handy,
      Below, the crew,
      All hit the brew,
          But the Capt'n swigged the brandy.

The Salem vamp wed a rich old scamp,
    While Phin was away rum runnin',
And they settled down in New York town,
    And the bride she was cute and cunnin'.
They lived a life of storm and strife,
    For the old bird was a blinger.
For many a shot by stealth he got,
    And every quaff a stinger.

Their honeymoon was over soon,
    For the rich bird was a bounder
Who blew his gold like a soak of old,
    For he was a rare old rounder.
And the *Nancy Lee*, she sailed the sea,
    And the air it was fresh and healthy.
And the Captain, proud, yelled orders loud,
    And he waxed enormous wealthy.

Chorus: Oh, blow, ye wild winds, blow,
        We'll fish no more from Glo'ster,
    For the lowly cod,
    And the simple scrod,
        Means nothing now to Foster.

Now, the widder's man conceived a plan,
    To buy it by the cargo,
And he made a deal where non would squeal,
    To dodge the dry embargo.
So the rich old bloke, he went stone broke,
    And although it may sound funny,
'Twas Capt'n Phin who run it in,
    And got all the old guy's money.

The vamp, of course, grabbed one divorce,
    When the old boy lost his boodle,
And he swigged this stuff that was awful tough,
    Till he went plumb off his noodle.
The Captain he gave up the sea,
    And a chorus girl, so smiley,
He up and wed, and now 'tis said,
    He's living the life of Riley.

Chorus: Oh, blow, ye wild winds, blow,
        Blow seven days a week,
    The vamp is back,
    In her Salem shack,
        And the Cap, is a Broadway Sheik.

Boston Herald, January 20, 1924

A Sailor's Chantey

Did you ever see a soldier with a lady on his arm?
    Oh, yes! It's not extremely rare!
Did you ever see a sailor who could not that lady charm?
    Oh, no! Providing he was there!
        For the sailor's eye is a roving eye
           That needs no prism glass,
      To get its proper focus
           When it's spying of a lass.

Chorus: Oh, the soldier's stock is rising,
           But the sailor heads his class!
    So a bunk upon the brine,
          Is good enough for mine,
    That's the reason I enlisted where
        The sea dogs whine!

Did you ever see a soldier looking lonesome as a fish?
    Oh, yes! The last one that I saw!
Did you ever see a sailor that you didn't hear a swish?
    Oh, no! And sometimes three or four!
        For the sailor's knot is a lover's knot
          That's tied in every port,
      It's a puny kind of Jackie who can't
          Capture what you've caught!

Chorus: Oh, there's something in his rolling gait,
           A soldier isn't taught!
    So a bunk upon the brine,
          Is good enough for mine,
    That's the reason I enlisted where
        The tide runs free!

Colorado Springs Gazette, September 9, 1918

The Great Lake Chantey

The Great Lake Chantey is a narrative or ballad chantey, which celebrates an event in the life of a particular seaman who composed it. This song was written by M.J. Powers himself, in commemoration of his last trip at sea a Great Lakes voyage.

In eighteen hundred eighty-seven,
    On the eighth day of June,
I shipped with Captain Jim Fleck,
    It was Wednesday afternoon.
He was a rattling old sailor man,
    Sometimes he could make a noise,
And we were bound away for Martin's Bay,
    In the schooner *A.P. Royce.*

When I went on board of that old boat,
    She looked like a total wreck,
But she's been put in the hands of the right man,
    When commanded by Old Jim Fleck.
He said, "We'll fit her out, my bully crew,
    For you have no other time or choice,
And you'll work all day in Martin's Bay,
    In the schooner *A.P. Royce.*

Now our mate being hard o' hearing,
    When the Captain he'd sing out,
"George, my lad, get ready,
    To put your ship about!"
Of course, he couldn't understand him,
    He had so low a voice,
And many's the job it saved the sailor lads,
    On the schooner *A.P. Royce.*

Three days we beat with a head wind,
    Until we made Green Bay.
We got a fair wind at Pilot Island,
    And then we squared away.
"Eat hearty now," the old man cried.
    "For we'll soon be at the ties."

"And it's all work and no play, In Marlin's Bay,
  On the schooner *A.P. Royce.*

When we went to put her deck-load on,
  The sun was mighty hot,
And every tie that we laid down,
  The old man cried, "Good Pot!"
"Good Pot," said I, "Oh, Captain dear,"
  "You know we are the boys,
That will take the bump*** out of the pot,
  On the schooner *A.P. Royce.*

It's when we had her loaded,
  It straightened out her hump,
He says, "My lads, we'll all make sail,
  And likewise man the pump.
You must keep her free, my bully crew,
  And we'll fetch Illinois,
You will pump night and day, if you want your pay,
  On the schooner *A.P. Royce.*

Plenty of provisions we had there,
  With an Irishman for cook,
He was just the lad that didn't care,
  If ye'd eat until ye'd choke.
Pies and puddings we had plenty,
  And of hash you had your choice,
You could eat away– but pump night and day–
  On the schooner *A.P. Royce.*

Three days we'd sail with a pleasant gale,
  Till we made the lighthouse dock,
It's then they commenced to discharge her poles,
  They were off at four o'clock.
Straightway we towed up the creek,
  For to discharge her ties,
And that put an end to my first trip,
  In the schooner *A.P. Royce.*

M.J. Powers, *New Orleans Item,* June 9, 1918

~ *3* ~

A Pirate's Life

Billy Bone's Fancy

Tune: *Blow the Man Down*

The first two lines of a song of West Indian piracy, which originated in the wreck of an English buccaneer on the day called *The Dead Man's Chest*, from which it is said only a quantity of rum and fifteen men were saved. For the complete song, which follows, I am indebted to Mr. Jeffery Montague of the *Richmond, Virginia Times*, who has pieced the various fragments of this song together.

Fifteen men on a dead man's chest,
    Yo, heave ho and a bottle of rum!
Drink and the devil had done for the rest,
    Yo, heave ho and a bottle of rum!

They drank and they drank and they got so drunk,
    Yo, heave ho and a bottle of rum!
Each from the dead man bit a chunk,
    Yo, heave ho and a bottle of rum!

They sucked his blood and they crushed his bones,
    Yo, heave ho and a bottle of rum!
When suddenly up came Davey Jones,
    Yo, heave ho and a bottle of rum!

And Davey Jones had a big black key,
    Yo, heave ho and a bottle of rum!
The key to his locker beneath the sea,
    Yo, heave ho and a bottle of rum!

He winked and he blinked like an owl in a tree,
    Yo, heave ho and a bottle of rum!
And grinned with a horrible kind of glee,
    Yo, heave ho and a bottle of rum!

"My men," says he, "you must come wi' me,"
    Yo, heave ho and a bottle of rum!
"Must come, wi' me to the depths of the sea,"
    Yo, heave ho and a bottle of rum!

So he clapped them into his locker in the sea,
    Yo, heave ho and a bottle of rum!
And he locked them in with his big black key,
    Yo, heave ho and a bottle of rum!

R.M.P. Jr., [Philadelphia] *Evening Public Ledger*, December 27, 1920

A Chantey of Wild Wives

"For Divorce Dubs Wife Loves Pirate," Headline.

Hoist up your standard, skull and bones,
    And make no bones about your standards;
Regardless of captives' means,
    Go boldly buccaneering man-wards.

Of weaker vessels take your toll,
    With firm pi-radical ideas;
For to the knave belongs the roll,
    Upon the rolling social seas.

"Seven men on a dead man's chest,"
    The ditty bold of lawless hearts,
You'll find a live man's bosun best,
    For practice of your pirate arts.

To make 'em pay, do not be loath;
    Hearts' ransoms always bring a high rate,
Just get a witness to their oath
    And treat 'em rough, an irate pirate.

Avoid the seashore, use the bank,
    To keep your buried treasure hid;
Just let your platform be a plank
    And be a clever little Kidd.

Carcass, *Chicago Daily News*, July 22, 1922

We're the Crew of Pierre Le Rouge

While he waited, the Guardsman extracted the parchment from his pocket and studied the latest of the strange puzzles, which Rupert believed would furnish the clue to the buried treasure. He shook his head sadly. His practical mind could not conceive that this strange combination of words and pictures could have any real meaning.

He did not have long, however, to consider this mystifying puzzle. Far down the hill, he heard the old hermit approaching – singing – singing a wild, bloodcurdling sea chantey of pirate days.

> We're the crew of Pierre Le Rouge,
> The Bloodiest crew that sails.
> The man who falls into our hands,
> With fear and terror pales.
>
> "We're on the trail of silver and gold,
> Doubloons and pieces of eight.
> He who defies our jet black flag,
> Will meet a bloody fate."

Buck shuddered; then his fear was quickly succeeded by alarm. Had the piratical old ruffian discovered the treasure? Was this a song of triumph – and of warning?

Knoxville News, April 6, 1934

The Gulf Chantey

"Yo-ho, yo-ho, and a rumbelow!
    And ho for the Spanish Main.
For the Devil has loosed his fiery leash,
    And we're off to Sea again!"
Then up they ramble, Captain Kidd;
    Lafitte and Black Beard, too.
And every wicked sailor man,
    That ever has worn a queue!

It's "Ho, my lads, the waves run high!"
    And "Sniff the salt sea breeze!"
"Lay off a point from the Spanish Reef,
    And make for the Caribbeea!"
"It's clear," say they, "there's the Devil to pay,
    When they summon the hosts of hell!"

Who sails to meet the grisly fleet?
    He flies the Union Jack!
It's Drake from Nombre Dies Bay,
    Where they sank him ages back;
And "Ha!" says he, "Will ye help a race,
    Nor oaths nor treaties hold?"
Then tales of murder, arson and lust,
    And the submarine, he told.

The tale of the sunken hospital ships,
    Or the Lusitania's drowned,
Deported millions, and starving hordes,
    And salt-sown harvest ground.
Cried Coxon: "It raises a seaman's gorge,
    When lies with canting mix!"
Quoth Morgan: "That gospel of frightfulness,
    Can teach the Devil new tricks!"

Lafitte he casts his eye above,
    To the Black Flag at his peak!
"By Bones and Skull, the measure is full;
    Let God His vengeance wreak!"
The cruel Don, and the Picaroon,
    Swore even we fought not thus!
So it's back to the gates of doom once more;
    No aid they'll get from us."

Says Cap'n Kidd as he turned his quid:
    "I vote we'll not go back;
For yon's no place, when that crew crowds in,
    For a self-respectin' Jack.
So yo-heave-yo, and ware the reef,
    Set sail and away we go!"
And the Devil he gave a sign of relief:
    For he needed their bunks below.

Alice Williams Brotherton, in the *New York Times*,
reprinted in *Baltimore American*, August 14, 1917

The Song of Captain Kidd

Roud No. 1900

The Original Words as They Were Sung in the Last Century.

To the Editor of the Inter Ocean:

In the American opera of *Sleepy Hollow*, which was lately given in this city, one of the fictitious pirates who so terrified Ichabod Crane, personated Captain Kidd and sang a few lines of the old song, which in the last century was as familiar all through New England as were the stories of his buried treasures along the coast. *Harper's Monthly*, for December, gives six stanzas of the same lugubrious ballad. It happened thirty-five years ago, when I was a boy a dozen years old, that I wrote down the entire ditty as below given, from the dictation of my great-uncle as he lay on his back with two canes beside him, toasting his rheumatic legs under the kitchen stove in my father's house on one of the hill-farms in Vermont. He sang the words to a mournful minor air, similar to the one adopted by *Sleepy Hollow* pirate, but not the same.

N.C.P.

Ye captains brave and bold,
    Hear our cries, hear our cries,
Ye captains brave and bold, hear our cries;
Ye captains brave and bold,
    Though you seem uncontrolled,
Don't for the sake of gold lose your souls.

My name was Robert Kidd,
    As I sail'd, as I sail'd,
My name was Robert Kidd, as I sail'd;
My name was Robert Kidd,–
    God's laws I did forbid,
And so wickedly I did, as I sail'd.

My parents taught me well,
   As I sail'd, as I sail'd,
My parents taught me well, as I sail'd,
My parents taught me well,
   To shun the gates of hell,
But 'gainst them did I rebel, as I sail'd.

I curs'd my father dear,
   As I sail'd, as I sail'd,
I curs'd my father dear, as I sail'd
I curs'd my father dear,
   And her that did me bear,
And so wickedly did swear, as I sail'd.

I made a solemn vow,
   As I sail'd, as I sail'd,
I made a solemn vow, as I sail'd
I made a solemn vow,
   To God I would not bow,
Nor myself one prayer allow, as I sail'd.

I'd a Bible in my hand,
   As I sail'd, as I sail'd,
I'd a Bible in my hand, as I sail'd,
I'd a Bible in my hand,
   By my father's great command.
And I sunk it in the sand, as I sail'd.

I murdered William Moore,
   As I sail'd, as I sail'd
I murdered William Moore, as I sail'd,
I murdered William Moore,
   And left him in his gore,
Not many leagues from shore, as I sail'd;

And being cruel still,
   As I sail'd, as I sail'd
And being cruel still, as I sail'd,
And being cruel still,
   My gunner I did kill.
And his precious blood did spill. As I sail'd;

My mate was sick and died,
   As I sail'd, as I sail'd
My mate was sick and died, as I sail'd,
My mate was sick and died,
   Which me much terrified,
When he called me to his bed-side, as I sail'd;

And unto me did say,
   See me die, see me die,
And unto me did say, see me die
And unto me did say,
   Take warning now I pray –
There comes a judgment day, see me die.

You cannot then withstand,
   When I die, when I die,
You cannot then withstand, when I die,
You cannot then withstand,
   The judgment of God's hand,
But bound in iron bands you must die.

I was sick and nigh to death,
   As I sail'd, as I sail'd,
I was sick and nigh to death, as I sail'd,
I was sick and nigh to death,
   And vow'd at every breath,
To walk in wisdom's path, as I sail'd.

I thought I was undone,
  As I sail'd, as I sail'd
I thought I was undone, as I sail'd,
I thought I was undone,
  That wicked glass was run,
But health did soon return, as I sail'd.

My repentance lasted not,
  As I sail'd, as I sail'd
My repentance lasted not, as I sail'd,
My repentance lasted not,
  My vows I soon forgot,
Damnation my just lot, as I sail'd.

I steer'd from sound to sound,
  As I sail'd, as I sail'd.
I steer'd from sound to sound, as I sail'd,
I steer'd from sound to sound,
  And many ships I found,
And most of them I burn's, as I sail'd.

I spied three ships from France,
  As I sail'd, as I sail'd
I spied three ships from France, as I sail'd,
I spied three ships from France,
  To them I did advance,
And took them all by chance, as I sail'd.

I spied three ships from Spain,
  As I sail'd, as I sail'd
I spied three ships from Spain, as I sail'd,
I spied three ships from Spain -
  I fired them on a main,
Till most of them were slain, as I sail'd.

I'd ninety bars of gold,
    As I sail'd, as I sail'd
I'd ninety bars of gold, as I sail'd,
I'd ninety bars of gold,
    And dollars manifold,
With riches uncontrolled, as I sail'd.

Then fourteen ships I see,
    As I sail'd, as I sail'd
Then fourteen ships I see, as I sail'd,
Then fourteen ships I see,
    All brave men they be;
They were too hard for me, as I sail'd.

Thus being o'er taken at last,
    I must die, I must die;
Thus being o'er taken at last, I must die,
Thus being o'er taken at last,
    And into prison cast,
And sentence being pass'd, I must die.

Farewell to the raging main,
    I must die, I must die,
Farewell to the raging main, I must die,
Farewell, the raging main,
    Turkey, France, and Spain,
I shall never see you again, for I must die.

To Newgate now I'm cast,
    And must die, and must die,
To Newgate now I'm cast, and must die,
To Newgate now I'm cast,
    With sad and heavy heart,
To receive my just desert, I must die.

To the Execution Dock,
    I must go, I must go,
To the Execution Dock, I must go,
To the Execution Dock,
    Will many thousands flock,
But I must bear the shock, and must die.

Come all ye young and old,
    And see me die, see me die,
Come all ye young and old, and see me die,
Come all ye young and old,
    You're welcome to gold,
For by it I've lost my soul, and must die.

Take warning now by me,
    For I must die, I must die,
Take warning now by me, for I must die,
Take a warning now by me,
    And shun bad company,
Lest you come to hell with me, for I must die.

[Chicago] *Daily Inner Ocean*, November 29, 1879

~ 4 ~

Drinking Songs, Prohibition

Grog Tune

Tune: *Battle Cry of Freedom* by George F. Root

The crew that shipped with him were usually good singers, and as they stayed with him year after year, they sang their chanties together very well. I remember parts of one of their songs, and I shall be grateful to you if you will print the whole of it and tell me who wrote it and how the music goes. I can hear the tune still, but being no hand at singing or even humming tunes, I can't get it out. They called it *Grog Tune*.

> When the captain wets his whistle,
> And the bosun serves the grog
> In the batter'd old tin dipper,
> While the mate consults the log.
>
> Chorus: Then rally round the capstan,
> And rally once again;
> There's nothing like *Old Medford* rum
> For thirsty sailor men.
>
> Come and join us in the chorus
> With lusty lungs and free;
> There were drinking men before us,
> There'll be drinkers after we.
>
> Chorus: Then rally round the capstan,
> And rally once again;
> There's nothing like *Old Medford* rum
> For thirsty sailor men.

I'm not sure whether "Jamaica" shouldn't stand instead of *Old Medford* in the third line of the chorus, and sometimes they said "mellow" for "thirsty" in the last line. In the Civil War we used to sing:

> "We'll rally round the flag, boys,
> We'll rally once again."

which is stolen boldly from the chorus. It is shameful that a patriot song should be written by a deliberate thief, isn't it? Do you know his name? Old Codger.

Boston Herald, March 25, 1918

Our Own Bootlegger Chantey

The bootlegger he is a lucky man,
   Sing Yo, Ho, Ho, for he certainly am,
For the tariff he don't give a damn,
   Sing Yo, Ho, Ho, in the morning.

He buys good rum and he fills his packs,
   He sells at the door of castles and shacks,
He never even heard of the income tax,
   Sing Yo, Ho, Ho, in the morning.

He gets his lead and brings it to a sign,
   That reads, "Near beer and apple cider wine,"
He laughs at laws and he thrives on crime,
   Sing Yo, Ho, Ho, all the time.

Springfield [Massachusetts] *Daily News*, October 21, 1922

Learn About Drinking From Me

When sailors go ashore on liberty, they head for the *Atlantic Cabaret* to renew old acquaintances and to drink to the longevity of new ones. It is not unusual to see a quartet of sailors on liberty for the day, engaged in nothing more than riding about the streets on a charted cab, and drinking from a keg between them.

There is a curious camaraderie existing among sailors and among soldiers, arising no doubt from the bonds of union, but more pronounced, perhaps by virtue of being in a strange land, the youngster observed. He spoke of brawls in which a horde of strange sailors swarmed to the aid of other strange sailors. With soldiers, it was similar.

Conviviality, however, is the rule most follow. Ralph recited a few verses he heard chorused from lusty ones out for a carouse.

> "I've taken my booze where I've found it,
>   From 'Frisco to Chesapeake Bay;
> Some were a dollar a throw, boys,
>   Some were a quarter for three.
> Some made me shout,
>   And made me pass out,
>   So hear about drinking from me."

> "I was drinking once with a Russian
>   In a low Petrograd bar,
> Just to show him I wasn't four-flushing.
>   We drank bottoms up to the Czar!
> Well, after one drink of that Vodka,
>   I was feeling my vision grow dim,
> As I rolled on the floor,
>   He was guzzling four more.
>   And I learned about drinking from him."

> "Next, I was drinking at Kelly's
>   With two good men by my side,
> I thought I was drinking fish cocktail,
>   And I felt like a clam at low tide.

But the drunkest I ever did get, boys,
    Was on old Epstein's gin, don't you see,
I was drunk for ten days,
    And I'm still in a haze,
        So learn about drinking from me."

Greensboro [North Carolina] *Record,* September 17, 1928

The Dry Chief's Chantey

Bootleggers, I fear not a single one,
    With my trusty gun at my side.
If they try to get me, I'll sure get them,
    And they'll die as they wish I had died.

And as for graft and taking their dough,
    Such talk gives me a pain.
As a private detective I earned more than now,
    And it seems that that ought to explain.

Now, the stuff they sell is poison stuff,
    And it rots a man's insides.
To take one cent for protecting such,
    By God, I've got more pride.

Duc D'Argyle, *New Orleans Item,* November 19, 1923

The Dead Men's Song

Fifteen men on a dead man's chest –
  Yo-ho-ho and a bottle of rum!
Drink and the devil had done for the rest –
  Yo-ho-ho and a bottle of rum!
The mate was fixed by the bos'n's pike,
The bos'n brained with a marlinspike,
And Cockney's throat was marked belike
    It had been gripped
      By fingers ten;
    And there they lay,
      All good dead me.
Like a break-o'day in a boozing-ken –
  Yo-ho-ho and a bottle of rum!

More was seen through the stern light screen –
  Yo-ho-ho and a bottle of rum!
Chartings no doubt where a women had been!
  Yo-ho-ho and a bottle of rum!
A flimsy shift on a bunker cot,
With a thin dirk slot through the bosom spot
And the lace stiff-dry in a purplish blot.
    Or was she wench…
      Or some shuddering maid…
    That dared the knife
      And that took the blade!
By God! She was stuff for a plucky jade –
  Yo-ho-ho and a bottle of rum!

Fifteen men on a dead man's chest –
  Yo-ho-ho and a bottle of rum!
Drink and the devil had done for the rest –
  Yo-ho-ho and a bottle of rum!
We wrapped 'em all in a mains'l tight
With twice ten turns of a hawser's bright,
And we heaved 'em over and out of sight –

With a yo-heave-yo!
And a fare-you-well!
And a sullen plunge
In the sullen swell.
Ten fathoms deep on the road to hell!
Yo-ho-ho and a bottle of rum!

No, Brother: They Won't Drink When They Have to Go to the Trouble
of Making it.

Sir– In publishing in your meritorious column a recipe for a dandelion
intoxicant, you are promoting the cause of intemperance. Jay Bee

Young E. Allison, *Harrisburg* [Pennsylvania] *Patriot*, May 29, 1919

Dry Navy Chantey

Tune: *Sailing, Sailing, Over the Bounding Main*

Sailing, sailing, over the bounding main,
When three miles out we out about,
    And sail right back again.

Skimming, skimming, over the restless sea,
A floating bar we sniff afar;
    We'd doubt a case of tea.

Rolling, rolling, over the ocean blue,
The ocean's wet, but ships, you bet,
    Are dry when we get through.

Tossing, tossing, over the drinkless brine,
We head for port, the kickful sort,
    Detect the lightest wine.

Cruising, cruising, three miles out from shore,
We seize their rum and still they come,
    With more and more and more!

Trenton Evening Times, July 5, 1922

Liverpool Rope

Tune: *Blow the Man Down*

I'll sing you a chantey, I'll sing you a song,
　Way! Hey! Blow the man down.
A song about rum, lads, so roll it along,
　Give us the time to blow the man down.

They've cut off our grog and they've cut off our beer,
　Way! Hey! Blow the man down.
When we go ashore it will make us feel queer,
　Give us the time to blow the man down.

The skipper will sing out when we are at sea,
　Way! Hey! Blow the man down.
"Serve to each man a full hooker of tea,"
　Give us the time to blow the man down.

Cursed be the man who has cut off our grog,
　Way! Hey! Blow the man down.
Making poor Jack lead the life of a dog,
　Give us the time to blow the man down.

A pipe and a glass are two jolly good pals,
　Way! Hey! Blow the man down.
They've cut off our grog, next they'll cut off the gals,
　Give us the time to blow the man down.

When we spin our yarns on the fo'c'sls head,
　Way! Hey! Blow the man down.
Yarns of the past, of sprees that are dead,
　Give us the time to blow the man down.

When we arrive on America's shores,
　Way! Hey! Blow the man down.
Dying of thirst we will broach the ship's stores,
　Give us the time to blow the man down.

When we get back to old Liverpool town,
Way! Hey! Blow the man down.
We'll drink day and night and do it up brown,
Give us the time to blow the man down.

Arthur Thornton, *New York Press*, March 23, 1919

Rum Chasers' Chantey

Our mighty fleet is under weigh,
We're off to dry the main
And cleanse the old Atlantic
Of its alcoholic stain.

We've bunched a great armada,
And we've "shaken up" each crew.
We think the boys remaining
Are dependable, if few.

So when we sight the enemy
Not many men will quail.
For our most doubtful Volsteaders *
Are left behind in jail.

And even if our Dries turn wet
Till none at all remain.
We'll sail back to our anchorage
And shake 'em up again.

Trenton Evening Times, May 8, 1925

[* Volstead Act aka National Prohibition Act. – RS]

Chantey of Notorious Bibbers

Oh, Homer was a vinous Greek, who loved the flowing bottle,
    Herodotus was a thirsty cuss, and so was Aristotle.

    Chorus: Sing ho! That archipelago
           Where mighty Attic thinkers
           Involved the grape to keep in shape
           And lampooned water drinkers.

King Richard fought the heathen Turk, along with his Crusaders,
    On wobbly legs that tippled kegs and hated lemonaders.

    Chorus: Sing ho! That gallant English King,
           Sing ho! His merry yeomen,
           Who felt the need of potent mead,
           To make them better bowmen.

Bill Shakespeare loved to dip his pen in Mermaid Inn canary,
    And Bobby B. was boiled when he indited "Highland Mary."

    Chorus: Sing ho! The buxom barmaid Muse
           Who did her work on brandy,
           She now eschews such vulgar brews
           And trains on sugar candy.

Dan Webster stoked his boilers with brown jugs of apple cider,
    And when he made a speech he yanked the spigots open wider.

    Chorus: Sing ho! Those spirited debates,
           Bereft of all restrictions,
           When statesmen carried on their hip
           The strength of their convictions.

Now pass the faucet water, lads, and pledge in melancholy,
   The simple ways of ancient days, for alcohol is folly.

   Chorus: Sing ho! That archipelago
                Where mighty Attic thinkers
                Involved the grape to keep in shape
                And lampooned water drinkers.

Let's live and grow on H_2O, and shun the lethal snicker,
   For records show that man below goes wrong by drinking likker.*

   Chorus: Sing ho! That archipelago
                Where mighty Attic thinkers
                Involved the grape to keep in shape
                And lampooned water drinkers.

Henry Morton Robinson, reprinted from the F.P.A.'s "Coming Tower,"
in the *New York World, Boston Herald,* July 1, 1927

[Changes noted are from *Life Magazine,* E.C. Perry, Jr., June 1932, p25,
Google books. The last two choruses were editorial additions not found
in the *Life Magazine* article. – RS]

The Uplift Sea

On reading that the sailor of today does not drink, swear nor chew tobacco.

Farewell to the old swinging chantey,
    To the hornpipe at last, long good-bye;
You may search near and far
For the old –fashioned tar,
    But today there just ain't such a guy.
Such expression as "Shiver my timbers!"
    Or "Belay!" or "Pipe down!" or "Avast!"
Which to you and to me
Gave a kick to the sea
    Have faded away in the past.

The seaman has gone in for culture,
    And, whether a-sea or ashore,
Profanity drips
From the blasphemous lips
    Of the fo'castle tenant no more.
His leisure is spent playing contract
    Or improving his flowering mind;
All the swaggering ways
Of his roistering days
    The sailor has left far behind.

Hereafter, the writers of fiction
    Whose heroes were hearty and bluff–
Who wore dungaree clothes
And used terrible oaths–
    Have got to revise all their stuff.
Though still is the mariner worthy
    To figure in story and song,
He's as gentle and mild
As a dear little child;
    The authors have got him all wrong.

James J. Montague, *Springfield* [Massachusetts] *Republican*, August 30, 1934

A Longshoreman Chantey

The longshoreman strikes for a dollar an hour,
   Now timber me toes, whittle me nose,
On an even three hundred the skipper grows sour,
   Now whittle me nose, timber me toes,

The half-baked young sailor wants ninety a mont',
   I'm tellin' no lies, batter me eyes;
At two hundred an' fifty the engineers grunt,
   Now batter me eyes, tellin' no lies.

But the clerk from the office on twenty a week,
   Now rattle me bones, laugh at me groans;
Come down to the dock lookin' happy and sleek,
   No heed to me groans, rattle me bones.

An' for nothin', less postage, contributors bright,
   They're less'n half bright, hammer me light,
Will torture their souls through half of a night,
   Yea, hammer me light, less'n half bright.

Twixt them as what gets it an' others as can't,
   It's plain to be seen, batter me bean,
That the good-tempered swabs as ye never hears rant,
   Now batter me bean, plain to be seen.

Of the high cost o' livin', the sorrow o' toil,
   Now step on me frog, kick at me dog,
Get the joy out o' life, I'm sore as a boil,
   THEY'VE CUT OFF ME GROG, CUT OFF ME GROG!

Ray Sargent, from the *N.Y. Tribune*, reprinted in the *Evening Journal*, October 30, 1919

~ 5 ~

Parodies

Billi Bumper

Tune: *Billy Taylor*

Letter to a Friend:

Dear M. – I hardly know what to write about, except I give you some idea of a sleigh ride, which just presents itself to my imagination – eight young ladies and gentlemen, with Timothy the fiddler, all bundle into one sleigh, with Jack Ropeyarn for the coachman, who had just got in from the sea, after a long cruise, and thought he'd take a commission in the land service, but who prudently did not show his colors till he got a good offering. Away they start – cold as Greenland – wind, blowing a gale – snow flying in their faces – get a mile or two – being rather dull, Jack whispers to Tim to strike up *Fishers Hornpipe* shipmate, and I'll give you the double shuffle here on the forecastle, for I'm getting rather cold. Oh! No! I'm 'fraid company won't like it.

Mr. Simper proposes a song – who shall it be? Mr. Chanta – Mr. Chanta will you favor us with one of your favorite songs? I would with great pleasure, but me te-te-teeth chat-chatters so with the cold, I can't do any song justice. Oh! That's a poor excuse, Mr. Chanta, they'll serve to help you out in the chorus, besides, Tim will strike up loodle, loodle, loo, and assist you through all the difficult parts. He pipes up to the tune of *Billy Taylor*.

> Billi Bumper was a jovial fellow,
>   Full of life and full of glee,
> Was turn's adrift by Nancy Bellow,
>   And drown'd himself right in the sea.
>
> His body soon was seen a floating,
>   Right before Miss Nancy's door,
> Soon as she saw the corpse approaching,
>   Loudly she began to roar.
>
> A shark got hold of Billy's garter,
>   Gave first a jerk and then a pull,
> Which set him up straight in the water,
>   Light and pale as any Gull.

Poor Nancy Bellow, quite distracted,
   In after Billi she gave a leap,
By which she soon the shark attracted,
   Who laid her with poor Billi to sleep.

Thank you, Mr. Chanta, very good song, never heard it before. Tim, strike up *Yankee Doodle*. Yes sir, Jacky shall I give it to 'm fast or slow? Oh! Give it to 'em three streaks upon deck, that's the number of strings to your fiddle, and I'll give you the double shuffle here on the forecastle, to keep myself warm.

Hartford Times, February 15, 1820

Cap'n Sears Kendrick

Tune: *Sally Brown*

The Book Factory by Edward Anthony:

Good contributions continue to arrive and crowd out our own stuff. For instance, this week we intended to top the column with some dialect verses we've written in High Wiley's rollicking new book *Lilly* and along comes Baron Ireland (who's been writing so much stuff for *The Saturday Evening Post* and *Life* that we didn't know he had time for us) with a merry column length review of Joseph C. Lincoln's *Fair Harbor* (written in the appropriate form of a sea chantey parody). We think we'll have to holler for more space or hereafter set the column in tiny ruby – a fitting type for our *Gems of Thought.*

By the way, Baron Ireland (whose ancestors were kings, queens, lords, dukes, & c.) tells us he sent us his poems in appreciation of the square deal we give royalty in our new book *The Pussycat Princess*. The Baron promises us a royal reception when we visit him at the ancestral caste in Caldwell, N.J. His poem follows:

> Cap'n Sears was a cap'n bold,
>> Way, oh, roll and go!
> He was thirty-eight years old.
>> Bet your money on Cap'n Sears.
>
> Cap'n he got in a railroad wreck,
>> Way, oh, roll and go!
> Busted his spars close down to the deck.
>> Bet your money on Cap'n Sears.
>
> Thought he never could be cured,
>> Way, oh, roll and go!
> What can't be cured must be endured,
>> Bet your money on Cap'n Sears.
>
> Thinkin' he no more would roam,
>> Way, oh, roll and go!
> Started to run an old ladies' home,
>> Bet your money on Cap'n Sears.

That was a job was far from merry,
    Way, oh, roll and go!
But he was sorry for Elizabeth Berry.
    Bet your money on Cap'n Sears.

Her mother was matron, but how she'd shirk!
    Way, oh, roll and go!
Elizabeth she done all the work.
    Bet your money on Cap'n Sears.

Cap'n Sears saved money and coal,
    Way, oh, roll and go!
A dam good manager, on the whole.
    Bet your money on Cap'n Sears.

Saved George Kent from bein' a crook,
    Way, oh, roll and go!
Saved most every one in the book.
    Bet your money on Cap'n Sears.

Finally Cap'n's legs got better,
    Way, oh, roll and go!
Married Elizabeth Berry, God bless her!
    Bet your money on Cap'n Sears.

Sailed away to foreign lands,
    Way, oh, roll and go!
Him and Elizabeth holdin' hands.
    Bet your money on Cap'n Sears.

Some of my lines rhymes kind of rankly,
    Way, oh, roll and go!
But you don't need rhymes in a dipsey chantey.
    Bet your money on Cap'n Sears.

Baron Ireland, *New York Herald,* November 11, 1922

Egbert Phillips

Tune: *Blow, Boys, Blow!*

Who do you think is the villain of her?
    Blow, boys, blow!
Egbert Phillips, the old maid lover,
    Blow, my bully boys, blow!

He p'tends he ain't mad as a barber,
    Blow, boys, blow!
Cause his wife left her money to found Fair Harbor,
    Blow, my bully boys, blow!

Oh, the whole dum town is in love with Phillips,
    Blow, boys, blow!
But he ort to be busted a whop with a skillet,
    Blow, my bully boys, blow!

He set the hull town by the ears,
    Blow, boys, blow!
An' he gits 'em mad at Cap'n Sears,
    Blow, my bully boys, blow!

He's awful slick an' insinuatin'
    Blow, boys, blow!
An' he gits George Kent to speculatin',
    Blow, my bully boys, blow!

He first makes up to Elizabeth's mother,
    Blow, boys, blow!
But he runs away an' marries another,
    Blow, my bully boys, blow!

Seein' he's him, that ain't so funny,
    Blow, boys, blow!
'Cause he found Elvira she had more money,
    Blow, my bully boys, blow!

But Cap'n Sears outwits the villain,
    Blow, boys, blow!
An' saves George Kent himself from killin',
    Blow, my bully boys, blow!

An' Cap'n marries Elizabeth Berry,
    Blow, boys, blow!
An' that's the end, so let's be merry!
    Blow, my bully boys, blow!

Baron Ireland, *New York Herald*, November 26, 1922

Tongues A-waggin'
Tune: *Fire Down Below*

Tongues a-waggin' fiercely,
    Tongues a-hangin' loose,
Tongues a-clackin' wildly,
    Clackin' like the duse.

Clackin', clackin',
    Clackin' all the time!
Fetch a couple o' gags,
    Clackin'! All the time!

Baron Ireland, *New York Herald*, November 28, 1922

Judah Cahoon

Tune: *Ranzo Was No Sailor or Reuben Ranzo*

Judah was no she cook,
    Pans, oh, boys, pans, oh!
Judah was a sea cook,
    Pans, oh, boys, pans, oh!

Here's to Judah's pans, oh!
    Pans, oh, boys, pans, oh!
Hurrah for Judah's pans, oh!
    Pans, oh, boys, pans, oh!

His face was full of whiskers,
    Pans, oh, boys, pans, oh!
His voice was full of blisters,
    Pans, oh, boys, pans, oh!

At the house of Ogden Minot,
    Pans, oh, boys, pans, oh!
He care took and was a pilot,
    Pans, oh, boys, pans, oh!

At Cap'n Kendrick's order,
    Pans, oh, boys, pans, oh!
He took him as a boarder,
    Pans, oh, boys, pans, oh!

The cookin' and the sweepin',
    Pans, oh, boys, pans, oh!
He done 'em, by the creepin',
    Pans, oh, boys, pans, oh!

The wood an' seaward haulin',
    Pans, oh, boys, pans, oh!
He done it, by the crawlen',
    Pans, oh, boys, pans, oh!

He sang a lot of chanteys,
  Pans, oh, boys, pans, oh!
That shocked Fair Harbor's aunties,
  Pans, oh, boys, pans, oh!

But Cap'n Sears would stop him,
  Pans, oh, boys, pans, oh!
Because he knew it shocked 'em,
  Pans, oh, boys, pans, oh!

And here this chantey closes,
  Pans, oh, boys, pans, oh!
By creepin', crawlin' Moses!
  Pans, oh, boys, pans, oh!

Oh, poor Judah's pans, oh!
  Pans, oh, boys, pans, oh!
Hurrah for Judah's pans, oh!
  Pans, oh, boys, pans, oh!

Baron Ireland, *New York Herald,* November 26, 1922

Oyster Time Chantey

He was a grizzled oysterman,
    From down the Chesapeake;
'Twas plain that he had rushed the can,
    Red was his sun-tanned beak.
He propped himself against the bar,
    His new found friends among,
And there and then the jovial tar,
    This chantey loudly sung.

"Oh! It's ho! For old Chesapeake Bay!
And it's ho! For the salt, salt spray;
    For the R-less months,
    Have done their stunts,
And now they've all gone away.
Sing ho! For the Chesapeake Bay!
    The oyster's king,
    Wherefore I sing,
This sweet little roundelay."

He bought the drinks with regal hand,
    He treated one and all,
Until the crowd could hardly stand,
    Against that grog shop wall.
He boasted of his pungey trim,
    He praised his sprightly crew,
He told of wealth in store for him,
    And then he shrieked anew:

"Oh! It's ho! For old Chesapeake Bay!
And it's ho! For the salt, salt spray;
  For the R-less months,
  When oysters hunt,
Are barred, have all flown away,
Sing ho! For the Chesapeake Bay!
  The oyster's king,
  And wealth he'll bring,
So we'll drink to him to-day."

Richmond Times Dispatch, September 3, 1916

A Wall Street Chantey

The J.P. Morgans pay no tax,
  Sing hey, sing ho, my hearties!
They keep cool millions frozen tight,
  Observant of each legal right,
And never lack for lawyers bright,
  Sing hey, sing ho, ho, ho!
But ah, the stock that Bill Jones gets,
  On beer and gas and cigarettes.
When he is to his ears in debts,
  Sing hey, sing ho, my hearties!

The J.P. Morgans have a knack,
  Belay, below, my bimbos!
A stock they can with rare skills take
  And into loss a profit make,
So income sleuths will cry, "All Jake!"
  Belay, below, oh, oh!
But Jones, with half pay cut 10 per cent,
  And half a house he cannot rent,
Finds loss accounts for him not meant,
  Belay, below, my bimbos!

Henry, *Springfield,* [Massachusetts] *Republican*, May 28, 1933

Deep Sea Chantey

"For the only ship that I ever saw was a partnership with my partner-in-law."— *Pinafore.*

My country called and I answered,
　　Thrilling in every nerve;
So I gave up my job and shipped as a gob
　　In Uncle Sam's Naval Reserve.

Oh, clean was the breath of the offshore wind,
　　And sweet was the scent of the offshore wind,
And the voice of the sea was alive in me,
　　And the tang of the brine in my heart.

Then they gave me the togs of a sailor,
　　And they shipped me to Pelham Bay,
And they taught me to chew as the sailor men do,
　　And to talk in a nautical way.

So I learned to scrub windows and hammocks,
　　And to carry a rifle on guard,
And to tell time by bells, and with pebbles and shells
　　To make anchors and things in the yard.

And the walls of our barracks were "bulwarks;"
　　When we spoke of the deck we meant "floor;"
And when, for example, we'd go out of camp,
　　We would say we were "going ashore."

And so, through the war's murk and darkness,
　　We valiantly stood at our post,
And never a gun of the venturesome Hun,
　　Was heard near the Westchester coast.

And never a U-boat reached Pelham,
    And never a Boche ventured nigh;
No shot ever fell upon fair New Rochelle,
    Mount Vernon, or Yonkers, or Rye.

And now I am back at my office,
    And my soul's crying out to be free,
For a tar nevermore can be happy ashore
    Who has harked to the call of the sea.

For, clean is the breath of the offshore wind,
    And sweet is the scent of the offshore wind,
And the voice of the sea is alive in me,
    And the tang of the brine in my heart.

Newman Levy, *New York Daily Tribune*, November 8, 1919

[Corrections based on *Gay But Wistful: Verses by Newman Levy*, Newman Levy,
Alford A. Knopf, New York, 1925, p66. – RS]

Sailor Song

There's a merry breeze, and a spreading sail –
  Heave-ho!
  And away we go!
With never a fear of the sweeping gale,
  Heave-ho!
  For the fresh winds blow!
There's a tender song in the ocean's roar,
And the chasing wind, as we fly before;
There are sweethearts waiting upon the shore,
  Heave-ho!
  And away we go!

There's a rolling path, that is wide and free –
  Heave-ho!
  And away we go!
There's a friend that ruleth the raging sea,
  Heave-ho!
  When the strong winds blow!
Or the tempest is rushing, fierce and fast,
By the shrieking cords and the bending mast,
There's a love that tempers the rising blast –
  Heave-ho!
  And away we go!

Our good ship's cleaving the ocean foam-
  Heave-ho!
  And away we go!
Over the billows, nearing home,
  Heave-ho!
  And the fresh winds blow!
Like the cheering ray of a midnight star
Is the beacon, glimmering free and far
From the haven, across the harbor bar-
  Heave-ho!
  And we homeward go!

J.H. Mackley, *The Cleveland Plain Dealer*, October 3, 1894

The Sea Scout's Chantey

This is a modern chantey, sung by crew of the sea scouts who took the famous pioneering trip up the Connecticut River in Government boats.

A ship is wood and metal,
  Is metal, rigging and sail,
She's but an iron kettle,
  When hearts aboard her fail!

Hauling Chorus: To my way-ay and yea, yea,
      We're bound away for many a day,
    A sea scout is a good scout,
      So give us our seaway.

The heart of ships is red-blood,
  Red-blood, never a doubt!
And wood and iron useless,
  Without the heart of scout.

Hauling Chorus: To my way-ay and yea, yea,
      We're bound away for many a day,
    A sea scout is a good scout,
      So give us our seaway.

Our ship is what we make her,
  Make her, saucy and smart.
No blustering wind shall break her,
  While we are all of a heart.

Hauling Chorus: To my way-ay and yea, yea,
      We're bound away for many a day,
    A sea scout is a good scout,
      So give us our seaway.

Chief Sea Scout James A. Wilder, *Judsonia* [Arkansas] *Weekly*, October 16, 1919

The Gulf of Mexico or
When the Winds Begin to Blow

I've heard them sing their chantey song,
　　Ye-ho, boys, ho!
But I like it better on the stage
　　Than where the billows flow,
For I've been out with sailor-men
　　Upon the deep blue sea,
And one good northern hurricane
　　Was quite enough for me.

　　　"Ye-ho, boys, ho!
　　　　When the wind begins to blow"!
　　　I'd rather hear it on the stage,
　　　　Than the Gulf of Mexico.

I love a good old chantey song,
　　And a hornpipe pleases me,
But I'd rather get them from the stage
　　Than a wind-tossed angry sea.
For I've pitched and tossed with Sailor-men
　　When the night was black as coal,
And I've no desire for a chantey song
　　When the ship begins to roll.

　　　"Ye-ho, boys, ho!
　　　　When the wind begins to blow"!
　　　I'd rather hear it on the stage,
　　　　Than the Gulf of Mexico.

For a day and a night we stood on end,
    First aft and then the bow,
And how we managed to stay afloat
    I don't remember now.
I only know that I had no taste
    For food and no ear for song,
And there's little joy in a chantey tune
    When the sea is running strong.

    "Ye-ho, boys, ho!
        When the wind begins to blow"!
    I'd rather hear it on the stage,
       Than the Gulf of Mexico.

Edgar Guest, *Houston Chronicle*, October 12, 1933

The Klondike Cow:
A Chantey of the North

Mush along you Malamutes,
    Hit the trail together,
Don't you see the little tykes,
    A-watchin' for their pa?
Mush along you wolf dogs,
    Before you feel my leather,
Got to make the shanty 'fore,
    They plumb wear out their run.
Grub on the sled,
    To fill their little tummies,
Won't they be happy,
    You can hear 'em laffin' low;
Best in the Northland,
    Is none too good, you rummies,
A case of real Carnation milk,
    The Klondike Cow.

Many years ago,
    I was perty skookum feller
Come to the Northland,
    A-lookin' for gold.
Over the Pass,
    We hunted for the yeller
Metal that we didn't find
    As thick as we'd been told.
Bacon and beans,
    A-cookin' on the embers,
Sourdough bread,
    The old prospector's chow;
Black coffee, too,
    How well I remembers
My first can of Carnation milk,
    The Klondike Cow.

'Twas over on the Tanana,
 When I was a packin'!
Grub for some Cheechakos,
 That had come across the hill,
Stopped for the night,
 And soon had a fire a-crackin',
Started in to eat,
 With a lot of room to fill,
Coffee in the tin cup,
 Like we always drink it,
Tenderfoot pulls out a can,
 Pokes two hole in the bow,
Pours out the real cream,
 A feller'd never think it
Would go so well – Carnation milk,
 The Klondike Cow.

Before very long
 In every camp and cabin,
Milk was as regular as bacon or as flour,
 Just take a can,
And your jackknife
 To jab in
A couple of holes
 And you've milk at any hour,
Along every trail
 You'll find these cans a-lyin'
Marks of the mushers,
 That have passed here, I 'low,
And never a man,
 Who have lived in the Northland
But's a friend of Carnation milk,
 The Klondike Cow.

Harold Otho Stone, *Anchorage Daily Times,* May 10, 1923

To the Heart of the Dead, Dead Calm

Resolute and *Shamrock IV* are wonders still, windless weather.
Yachtsmen's dope.

Sing hey for the strife in the sailor's life
    And ho for the ocean blue!
Apportion praise for the sun's bright rays
    And the clouds that they filter through.
But of all of the glee from the port to lee
    There's none to compare as balm

To the skipper's hopes, as he eyes his ropes,
    To the heart of the dead, dead calm! Yo, ho!
      To the heart of the dead, dead calm!

For bards may prate of the tossing gait
    Of a craft in a scudding breeze,
And the splashing foam of a race to home,
    And the like antiquities!
But it's naught they know of the stately flow
    Of the ships that never mind

A single snare in the summer air
    Save the puff, of a faint, faint wind!! Yo, ho!
      Save the puff, of a faint, faint wind!

Oh, his hopes are high for whatever sky
    Or the boundless main may bring!
For he scoffs at fog and his agile log
    Will whiss like anything.
But the boss of the sails full well bewails
    His luck and a nasty turn,

When his art's denied and his skill belied
    By a stiff, stiff breeze a-sters! Yo, ho!
      By a stiff, stiff breeze a-sters!

M.T.C., [Philadelphia] *Evening Public Ledger*, July 17, 1920

"Paddy" Noisiest and Best

Off Rosebank, S.I., lies an old United States Naval vessel which was used through the war as a guard boat for New York Harbor. It was there in the summer of 1917, that I first knew "Pop" McKinney, Bosun's Mate. He was old and brown and small, and scarred by the storms of fifty years at sea. All day long he growled at our clumsy landlubber ways, and our abysmal ignorance of bowlines and marline and hambroline. But at night, when the wind came cool off the sea, and the blinker lights winked on Fort Hamilton, and we could hear voices, and the barking of dogs and city sounds from shore. Pop would join our circle topsides about the galley hatch and growl and cough, and wonder if maybe we'd like if he would sing a bit. They were wonderful songs he sang, and we all learned them, too., and roared them out together across the flooding tide. Best and noisiest of all was "Paddy."

I was in London in the cold months of December,
   And all my money I had spent,
Oh, how it went today I can't remember,
   But I down unto a shipping office went.

    Chorus: Paddy go whack, take in the slack,
           And heave away the capstan,
        Heave a pull, heave a pull,
           For we're bound, ship staysails, boys be handy.

In those days there was a great demand for sailors,
   From London around Cape Horn and back to France –
So I shipped me aboard of a bark they called the *Oxford*,
   Oh, here's to take a drink to my advance.

    Chorus: Paddy go whack, take in the slack,
           And heave away the capstan,
        Heave a pull, heave a pull,
           For we're bound, ship staysails, boys be handy.

San Antonio Light, January 28, 1919

Oh! The Gertrude Steer!

Air: *The Bold Privateer*

The most diabolical and incomprehensible production that was ever concocted in the way of a slang song, however, is probably the following, which is sold by the ballad publishers here.

Oh! the *Gertrude* sloop is a bully sloop,
 She's a yacht from her keel, she's a yacht to her poop;
When her boom swings around, it swings with a swoop
 That knocks every muffin-head what don't stoop!

Strong Chorus: Oh! the *Gertrude Steer!*
   And keep her clear
   Of the big boats and the shad nets
   In the North Rivyear!

Oh! the *Gertrude's* crew is the bestest crew
 That ever sailed a vessel on the water blue;
For the bold and staunch and round and true,
 Is the heart of each Hearty in the Gertrude's crew.

Very Strong Chorus: Oh! the *Gertrude Steer!*
   And keep her clear
   Of the big boats and the shad nets
   In the North Rivyear!

Oh! our spree on the sloop is the darndest spree
 That ever was had on land or sea;
For we are bully boys, very bullie,
 But the bulliest boy in the crowd is Me!

Rather Stronger Chorus: Oh! the *Gertrude Steer!*
   And keep her clear
   Of the big boats and the shad nets
   In the North Rivyear!

We have enough to eat, for we don't keep a Cox-
    There are pipes and tobacco in that old tin box;
If any more is wanted, just climb up the rocks,
    And coax it from the gir-ruls in the snow-white frocks.

More Stronger Chorus: Oh! the *Gertrude Steer!*
        And keep her clear
      Of the big boats and the shad nets
        In the North Rivyear!

There's not such a thing as a quarter, Oh!
    On any foul monster in the *Gertrude*, no!
And if there was we'd sink it low
    In lager bier and Deutscher Schneider wine Rhine-O!

Irrepressible Chorus: Oh! the *Gertrude Steer!*
        And rise a cheer
      With a tiger and a bulldog,
        On the North Rivyear!

Sounds of cheers, tigers, whoops, cat-calls and other dulcet operations.

The remarks "for we don't keep a Cox" has reference to the memorable steward on board the *Great Easter*, when that steamer made the excursion trip to Cape May from this city [New York] some three years ago. He was made immortal for the way in which he starved the passengers.

New York Daily Post, October 22, 1863

Sea Chantey

Occasioned by reading that swearing at members of the crew is frowned on by several transatlantic lines.

The bosun sat on a capstan, aft,
   Blow, bullies, blow.
Sometimes he cried and sometimes he laughed
   Til the captain said he'd gone plumb daft,
And the mate hid under the port life raft,
   With, a yo, heave, yo.

Then the bos'n took him a shot of grog,
   Wind the anchor 'round.
And he threw his boot at the taffrail log,*
   And a marlinspike at the carpenter's dog,
And he called the ship's cook a polly-wog. **
   Now we're Rio bound.

"Oh, man and boy, I've sailed the sea,"
   Hear the trade winds blow.
"Since Eighteen Hundred and Sixty-three,
   But this is the worst I ever see,
When a man can't cuss the crew," sez he.
   Let the tiller go.

"Now, what'll they do on a dusty day,"
   Johnnie's in the scupper.
"When the seas are steep and the sky is gray,
   Will the bosun turn out the crew and say,
'I'll show some work to do, if I may;"
   Duff *** and ox for supper.

With that he took him a mighty chaw,
   Over the line she goes.
And the sailor shivered at what they saw,
   But the captain only said, "Oh pshaw."
(Which some of the crew thought pretty raw.
   Hold 'er on 'er toes.)

Sailin' her easy across the line, ****
    Blow, bullies, blow.
Winds are fair and weather's fine,
    And the sailor's life is free from care,
For the bos'n simply must not swear.

Paul Bungan, *Seattle Daily Times*, August 12, 1927

[* A two-part mechanical log that is towed astern and measures a
    vessel's speed and registers the distance traveled though the water. — RS]
[** An inexperienced sailor. — RS]
[*** A flour pudding boiled or steamed in a cloth bag. — RS]
[**** The line referring to the Equator, where an initiation turns a
    polly-wog into a shellback. — RS]

Canaday I.O.

One lovely summer's evening, on the 13th of July,
    'Twas a beautiful young maiden that I happened then to spy,
I said to her, "My Mary Ann, just promise me you'll go,
    And I'll take you to that pretty place called Canaday I.O."

    Refrain: Then blow, ye winds of a mornin',
            I care not how ye blow;
       And it's blow ye winds of the mornin' in
       Canaday I.O.

O, I went to Queen Victoria, and I took her by the hand,
    And I said to her, "Just tell me now, how does ould Ireland stand;"
She gave some good advice to me, that I'll always bear in mind,
    And she talked to me so pleasantly and was so very kind.

    Refrain: Then blow, ye winds of a mornin',
            I care not how ye blow;
       And it's blow ye winds of the mornin' in
       Canaday I.O.

She said, "Young man, I like your style, and now you must keep cool,
    For old Ireland shall have liberty and likewise have home rule;"
O, I thanked her very kindly in a voice so sweet and low,
    As I started for that pretty place called Canaday I.O.

    Refrain: Then blow, ye winds of a mornin',
            I care not how ye blow;
       And it's blow ye winds of the mornin' in
       Canaday I.O.

O, I married the pretty maiden, and we're on our little farm;
    And it's may you be as lucky boys, and guarded from all harm.
O, the reason I'm so happy now, tis just like this, you know,
    For my Mary Ann is with me now, in Canaday I.O.

Refrain: Then blow, ye winds of a mornin',
        I care not how ye blow;
        And it's blow ye winds of the mornin' in
        Canaday I.O.
            'BLUE JEANS'

Sunday Times, [Michigan] *Bay City Times,* January 19, 1902

A Life on the Ocean Wave

Tune: *A Life on the Ocean Wave*
Roud No. 31316

Not So Bad, At That

Captain Foldat and Bob Chesney and Jack Pennington and other handy Vikings that guide the destinies of the streamer *Wapama* up and down the coast used to tell me a few trips back what a hard hard life the sailorman has, never sticking in one port long enough to get homesick when he leaves it again, and all that.

And then-ah-then, the *Wapama* came rolling into St. Helens and we got a paper and found that Oregon had gone bone-dry.

And so I reached for my kettledrum and trolled the following deep-sea chantey, just to show the captain, Bob, and Jack how much sympathy they get from me.

A life on the ocean wave,
   A home on the rolling deep,
Where she, pitches when you shave,
   And she tosses when you sleep!
Oh, a sailor man may fret
   And a sailor man may sigh-
But a lot of the ports are wet,
   Through a lot of the ports are dry.

Chorus: A life on the ocean wave,
        A home on the rolling deep,
       Though you sometimes kick and rave,
        Sure, I envy you a heap.

Supposin' you had to stay
   In a dry Northwestern port?
You'd have a good right to say
   That sailing's a dreary sport,
Like an eagle caged, I pine
   In the Port of Portland here–
While you're off o'er the heaving brine
   To the city of the tall steam beer.

Chorus: A life on the ocean wave,
A home on the rolling deep,
Though you sometimes kick and rave,
Sure, I envy you a heap.

Your stay in the ports is brief
And you leave in a little while,
Which you say is a cause for grief,
But I think is a cause to smile.
For the Northern coast is bleak
For a long, long stop, I think,
But you never are more than a week
From a place you can get a drink.

Chorus: A life on the ocean wave,
A home on the rolling deep,
Though you sometimes kick and rave,
Sure, I envy you a heap.

A life on the ocean wave,
A home on the rolling deep;
Ah, Jack, you may kick and rave,
But I envy you a heap.
Like an eagle caged I pine
In the dry belt day by day-
And you're off o'er the heaving brine,
Round for wet San Pedro Bay.

Chorus: A life on the ocean wave,
A home on the rolling deep,
Though you sometimes kick and rave,
Sure, I envy you a heap.

Oregonian, December 12, 1916

~ *6* ~

Miscellaneous
Songs

Jimmy Yole's Chantey

Cast Teeth in Sea; They Come Back
———————————————
Yeth – with Quahogs –
Jimmy Yole Yodels
Cheery Chantey

Come all ye quahog fishermen
And listen unto me
And I'll tell you of the rescue
Of my false teeth from the sea.

New Bedford, Mass., Jan 18 – Jimmy Yole, member of the crew of the powerboat *Roland M.*, just back from the grounds, is entertaining all his brave mates of the quahog fleet with his new chantey. Jimmy is yodeling blithely, for his store molars are safe once more in their haven of refuge.

Jimmy was below and peeling onions when he became seasick. Presently, he ran on deck and leaned over the rail. His artificial teeth went over the side. Jimmy returned to his work.

Capt. Viv Forge started up the engine and began to operate the dredges over the quahog ground. When the sixth scoopful came aboard the men on deck uttered a tremendous shout. Jimmy, alarmed, came racing from the cabin and saw something gleaming against the dark background of bay mud. Yeth, there they wath-hith teeth! So Jimmy concludes his chantey:

So all ye old quahoggers
You must never, never fail,
To take out all your store teeth
Before you breast the rail.

For Davy Jones's locker
Is a very deep, deep, hole,
And you may not be as lucky
As was your Jimmy Yole.

Boston Herald, January 19, 1926

Who Go Down to the Sea in Ships

Above the brim of the crystal goblet,
   Where the rosy nectar drips,
I give this toast to the gallant sailors,
   Who go down to the sea in ships:

"Yea Ho! Yeo Ho! When the anchor raises,
   As the straining cable slips,
Here's a parting health to the fearless sailors,
   Who go down to the sea in ships."

Oh, near or far, on the crested billow,
   Where the wide-winged sea bird dips,
There is the home of the roving sailors,
   Who go down to the sea in ships.

When the tide comes in from the outer ocean,
   Then I sing, with glowing lips,
The lilting song of the happy sailors
   Who go down to the sea in ships.

Mrs. Sharlie F. Acree, *Houston Post,* April 4, 1926

An Off Shore Chantey

The oft-repeated swan song of a Deep Sea Lover.

> Ho! Yo! Home with sheet an' bowlin',
>> Flatten braces in a bit,
>>> She's leanin' to it now.

> Hi! Yi! Sweethearts, we're a-strollin',
>> We'll kiss you when we come back if,
>>> You ain't forgotten how!

> Hi! Yi! Bend your back, you lubber!
>> H'ist your wheel a spoke or two,
>>> An' give her a good full.

> Yo! Ho! Riggin's made o' rubber,
>> You can stretch it if you try,
>>> So Pull, Pull, Pull!

> Ho! Yo! Leavin' wine an' women,
>> Never seen much wine in mine,
>>> But rum's the stuff to burn.

> Hi! Yi! Sweethearts, we'll come swimmin',
>> And if you have forgotten,
>>> Why, there's others we can learn!

> Yi! Hi! Put your helm hard over,
>> Tack her once, then coffee, lads,
>>> An' no more cakes for tea.

> Yo! Ho! Pointin' out by Dover,
>> No more damned, jammed land for us,
>>> We're makin' out to sea.

Rowland Thomas, in *American Magazine*,
reprinted in *Omaha World Herald*, March 11, 1910

High Water Chantey

O saucy tug, your snort and chug
    Drive all our bridges skyward.
Know you how rude your nerve is viewed,
    Your name become a by-word?
No other town of like renown,
    Poor tolerant Chicago,
Would give you grace to show your face,
    Or stand your raw bravado!

We wonder much; your manners such,
    You never pause to ponder...
While millions wait your careless gait,
    Up on the highway, yonder,
O tug, your path leads on to wrath...
    Lord help you, is the passion
Of those you balk, who ride or walk,
    Adopt your arrant fashion!

Arthur Sheekman, *Chicago Daily Times*, September 19, 1929

Chantey

A wet sheet and a straining sail,
    And a sea of shifting blue,
A wide sky and a rousing gale,
    And joy in the heart of you;
A clean line, where the sky hangs low,
    And a seagull soars and dips;
And the old voice that bids men go —
    Go down to the sea in ships.

So go and sail the gold sea,
    The bold sea, the cold sea,
The waving, craving, raving sea,
    That fringed with silken foam.
Oh, go and sail the green sea,
    The keen sea, the mean sea —
But if it's all the same to you,
    I'll stick around at home.

The swift turn of the night wind's whim,
    And the twang of hempen strings;
The sharp snap of the halyards slim,
    And the spray that cuts and stings.
The wild chorus the breezes hum,
    And the waves that prowl and creep;
And the old voice that bids men come —
    Come over the tameless deep.

So go and sail the White Sea,
    The light sea, the bright sea,
The dashing, crashing, smashing sea,
    That dances in the gale.

Go on and sail the sad sea,
 The bad sea, the mad sea —
But if it's just the same to you,
 I'd rather be in jail.

     Dorothy Parker, [Michigan] *Adrian,*, May 4, 1925

[Corrections from: *Not Much Fun: The Last Poems of Dorothy Parker*, updated
with newly found material. Stuart Y. Silverstein, Scribner Publishing, 1996,
p118. -- RS]

Dover Chantey

The chalk cliffs of Dover,
 They run down to the sea,
And the little ladies scrubbin'
 Them nice and white with rubbin',
They call and call the rover:
 "Come back, come back to me!"

The pale cliffs of Dover,
 Light forth the dark patrols;
The waves laugh in the scuppers,
 "We've got em on their uppers;
Their 'Tag' will soon be over,
 God shrive their bloody souls!"

The white cliffs of Dover,
 They must our gravestone be,
Right thru the bow we stove 'er,
 O Merry Dun o' Dover,
We'll sign with you off Dover,
 To ship down in the sea!

   Terry, *Rock Island Argus and Daily Union*, December 1, 1921

Canine Chantey

The dog-muzzling ordinance is to be repealed. —News Item.

All over the city, with gay intonation,
　　While thousands of tails are with gaiety swaying,
The song of the canine in glad exultation,
　　Runs through the whole gamut of jubilant baying:
　　　　For the City Commission
　　　　Assumes the position,
For which all the doggies for months have been wishin',
　　And woe from the life of the canine disposes,
　　　　For soon will the muzzles be off of their noses.

The heart of the spitz and the pointer and setter,
　　The collie, the dachshund and bench-legged bulldog,
Leaps up like a prisoner freed from his fetters,
　　Till every dog with pure joy is a full dog;
　　　　For their bondage is ended,
　　　　And they are befriended,
Humanity's efforts for them are expended,
　　And they frolic about in exuberant poses,
　　　　For soon will the muzzles be off of their noses.

Wide swing the gay tails, as they think of the clearance,
　　The solving at last of that intricate puzzle
Of how to snap fleas, with the base interference,
　　That man has forced on them in form of a muzzle.
　　　　For freedom is rending
　　　　Their fetters, and ending
The bondage in which many months they've been spending,
　　And paradise freely her portals uncloses,
　　　　For soon will the muzzles be off of their nose.

Dean Collins, *Portland Oregonian*, November 21, 1914

A Deep Sea Chantey

Ye ho! The wind is nor' by so' by so' by east by west,
　　There's a luff abaft the scuttlebutt an' in the galley chest,
The fore-top-gallant marlin-spike is loo'ward of the rail,
　　It's ho my bullies,
　　　　Hi my bullies, reef the anchor brail!

Ye ho, the garboard* strake is gone, the mizzen poop is free,
　　The mainspring of the starboard watch is sinkin' in the sea,
Clew down the royal foc's'l bitts, belay the flukes, belay!
　　It's ho my bullies,
　　　　Hi my bullies, rollin' down the way.

Ye ho, the spanker spanks the lifts; the vangs are on the jib,
　　The weather sky-s'l braces are a whangin' down the bib,
Abeam, Abeam, the stuns'lls clash against the capstan keys,
　　It's ho my bullies,
　　　　Hi my bullies, jibs her to the breeze!

Hard down, hard down, the davits pull, the gunnels flap an' roll,
　　The maintop's in the booby hatch, ware shoal, ye scum, ward shoal!
She's westing so' by east by nor', ye ho, my lads, ye ho!
　　We'll sing a deep-sea chantey now,
　　　　Hi bullies, let her go!

Berton Braley, *San Antonio Light*, February 23, 1923

[You think my deep-sea terms are wrong?
　　I rather thought you might,
But they'll mean just as much to you
　　As though I had them right! — B. B.]

Sponger Money
or The Key West Chantey

One of the little-known and very complete books about Florida and Key West is *Palmetto Country*, by Stetson Kennedy. Kennedy is married to a Key West girl. He has an amazing amount of research. For instance, here's *Sponger Money*, well know *Key West Sea Chantey*:

Sponger money never done, sponger money,
  Look at my hand, my hand look new,
Cause I don't want no other money
  But sponger money.

Look in my trunk and see what's street, sponger money,
  One hundred dollars was my share, sponger money,
I'm gonna take away your woes, sponger money,
  I'm gonna buy you fine new clothes, sponger money.

Then when we go out on the street, sponger money,
  You'll be lookin' nice and neat, sponger money,
Then all the boys will envy me, sponger money,
  Then all the girls will fall for me, sponger money.

Money don't make me, you know, sponger money,
  Sponger money ever flow, sponger money,
Tell ev'ry body in town, sponger money,
  Me and my gale gonna dance 'em down, sponger money.

Sponger money never done, sponger money,
  Cigarmakers on the bum, sponger money,
But I'll treat just the same, sponger money,
  Keep them boys from feelin' shame, sponger money.

Look in the corner, see what's there, sponger money,
  Champagne, whiskey, gin and beer, sponger money,
Tell everybody that you see, sponger money,
  We're gonna have a shivaree, sponger money.

Key West Citizen, December 31, 1945

A Riverside Drive Chantey

Give me the open sea, sailing under Peary,
    Farragut or Febiger or Francis Drake!
Troll a lay of Baffin's Bay, Michigan or Erie,
    Huron or Superior or some such lake.

Put me under Captain Dunn or even General Harbord!
    Let me hear the chanteys that the seamen sing!
Oh, to slack a leeward tack and jibe her hard-a-starboard!
    And, oh, the lass is lovely when the fog bells ring!

How I crave the cruel wave and the billow bounding!
    How I love the capstan and the marlinspike!
But the jargon of the tar, the nautic note resounding,
    Best of all about the sea are what I like.

Mine a home upon the foam, on pinnaces* or cattleships!
    This, my hearty lubbers, is the sort of thing,
I can write when all the night the River's full of battleships,
    Keeping me from slumber when the fog bells ring.

New York Daily, October 20, 1920

[* A small boat, with sails or oars, forming part of the
    equipment of a warship or other large vessel. — RS]

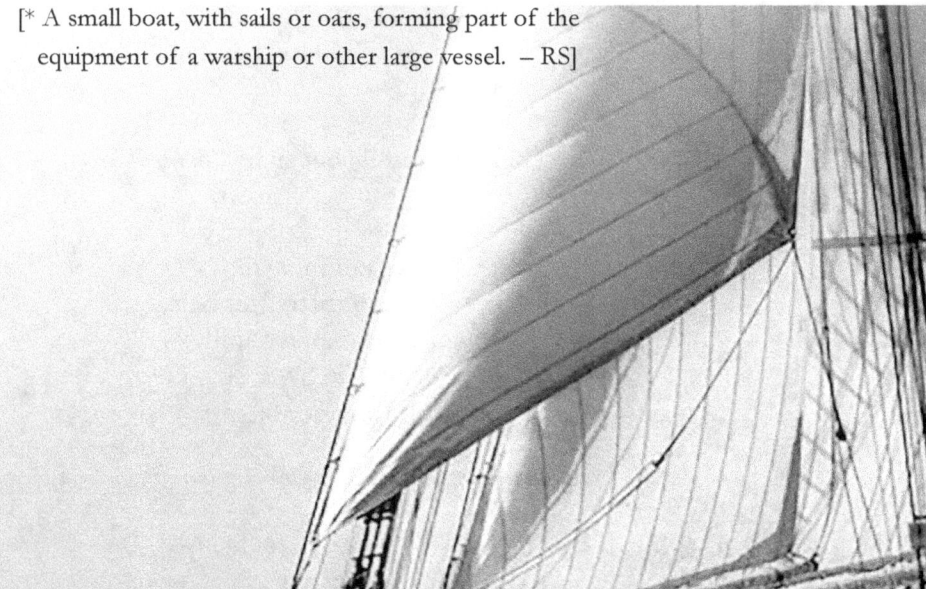

Goin' Fishin'

Keep steddy, boy, an haul away—
    We've got a dandy school,
When fish is like they are today,
    We've got to take 'em cool.
Suppose ye be some hungry, lad,
    Jes, now that ain't no sign;
Ye wouldn't mention grub, 'f ye had
    A halibut on yer line.

Waal, this is sumpthin like, I vow,
    I hope we'll swamp the boat!
Don't look so skeered! I guess the scow
    Won't de no worse'n float.
That's well! You really beat the Detch;
    That cod is extra fine!
Now pay her out ag'in and ketch
    A halibut on yer line.

I'll l'arn ye, if I kin, the way
    To gaff the largest ones;
So git a lot o' line to pay,
    No odds how far it runs.
An when ye feel a mighty haul—
    By jingo! There goes mine!
The Satan grabbed my bait an all—
    A halibut on my line.

There, now, I'll shet right up, an you
    Must do the bes' ye kin;
I'll bait another hook or two
    Ands cast 'em in ag'in,
I giss it's bes' to throw yer bait
    An set an hump yer spine—
You've got to watch yer chance, an wait,
    Fer halibut on yer line.

Yankee Blade, *Canton* [Ohio] *Repository*,, February 2, 1893

A Tip From the Cook in the Galley

So, at the Naval Training Camp here, they sing—morning, noon and night, over their clothes washing at daylight and in their tents in the evening, whenever two sailors get together, somebody starts like this:

> If you don't like the chow that we're having,
>   If you don't like the old slum gullion,*
> Then go back to your knife, fork and spoon,
>   But take a tip from the cook in the galley,
> Go take a flying jump at the moon!

Seattle Daily Times, June 23, 1918

[* A vile is a worthless person. -— RS]

An Amateur Chantey

> I sing a salty song,
>   A bluff and breeze stave,
> Of winds that whistle strong,
>   Of wicked, white-fanged wave.
>
> I sing about the wash
>   Of green sea o'er the rail,
> The rolling, tossing, Gosh,
>   The idea turns me pale.
>
> If I were on the sea,
>   'Twould be a different thing,
> My appetite would flee,
>   I know I couldn't sing.

John McColl, *New Orleans Item*, September 27, 1918

The Telephonic Sea Chanties

Tune: *Ten Thousand Miles Away*

News Item – Now possible to phone ships at sea.

A wet sheet and a flowing sea,
  A wind that follows fast
And fills the white and rustling sail
  And bends the gallant mast;
And bends the gallant mast, my boys,
  While like... oh, pardon me...
I hear the phone bell ringing and
  I guess the call's for me.

Oh for a soft and gentle wind!
  I heard a fair one cry;
But give to me the howling breeze
  And white waves heaving high;
And white waves heaving high, my boys,
  The good ship ... damn it all!
That phone is ringing once again,
  I'll have to take the call.

There's tempest in the horned moon
  And lightning in yon cloud,
And hark the music, mariners
  The wind is piping loud;
The wind is piping loud, my boys,
  Oh, listen to its moan...
I would but I must answer, boys,
  The blank-blank telephone!

H.I. Phillips, *New Orleans Item*, December 19, 1929

A Roving Wrecker's Chantey

I've had my fill of wrecking,
  Tearing up the bricks,
Scraping up the mortar,
  Loading up the sticks:

I've had my fill of wrecking,
  In spite of all the pay,
A juicy three and fifty,
  For a nine-hour day:

I've had my fill of wrecking,
  The boss and I, you see,
That g****** ****** foreman
  And I could not agree:

For I was there to sun myself,
  So jolly and so free,
An not to break my fragile back.
  For the Symons' Company.

Art Shields, *New York Daily Worker*, May 7, 1927

[* Offensive language — RS]

Chantey Bill

I am hearin' Chantey Bill,
    Above th' talkin' waters;
His bellow splits th' shadows of
    Th' years that have long passed;
He is yo-heave-ho-in,
    As we're takin' up th' anchor.
An' th' clipper, like a tremblin' colt, gets under way at last.

I can see th' strainin' crew
    That Chantey Bill is leadin'
With his "Roll 'er bullies!
    Roll the cotton down!"
Tanned an' singin' seamen,
    Grinnin' at their labors.
Dreamin' of the girls that they are leavin' back in town.

"There are dames a-waitin'!"
    Old Chantey Bill is shoutin'
"Roll an' go, my bullies!
    Roll 'er 'round an' go!"
An' the laughin' seamen,
    Th' sons of forty seaports,
Set the skies to rearin', with their "Yo-heave-ho!"

I am hearin' Chantey Bill,
    Although I know he's sleepin'
In a cave of coral,
    At the bottom of th' sea;
I'm old an' yet I'm hearin'
    Chantey Bill yo-ho-in.
An' I'm thinkin' the Great Skipper, is a-summonin' of me.

San Diego Union, June 6, 1926

Whaler's Chantey

We've said good-bye to our dearies,
　　We've laid tobaccy in store,
We're startin' a three-year whalin' cruise,
　　From Hell to Singapore;
The wind is over the quarter,
　　The banks are under the lee,
Heave-O! Tail on to a sheet!
　　We're standin' out to sea!

Her fo'c's'le's painted with whitewash,
　　Her hold is pumped out dry,
There's empty barrels atween decks,
　　An' the boats are nested high.
There's maybe a thousand fish to catch,
　　An' a lump of ambergree,
An' the ol' tub carries a bone in her teeth,
　　A-snorin' down to sea!

There's gals a-plenty in Boston,
　　Will moor you if they can,
But seldom a gal can ride it out,
　　With a rovin' sailorman.
Oh, the wind is over the quarter,
　　The banks are under the lee,
Heave-O! Tail on to a sheet!
　　We're standin' out to sea!

The King of the Black Isles, *Boston Herald,* April 7, 1923

A Dipsea Chantey

"Sponges are heartless creatures."– Bulletin of Natural History Museum.

We is cruisin' away from Whalebone Bay,
    And I'm snatchin' a wink o' sleep,
When I falls on my neck from the orlop deck,*
    And lights in the briny deep.
And I shoots below twenty fathom or so–
    Oh, that were a terrible plunge!
Then I opens my eyes with a shocked surprise–
    I'm aboard of a giant Sponge.

I makes a leg, and I start to beg,
    His pardon for this here call;
I was out o' breath and scared to death,
    And I scarcely could move at all.
I ast for jest a minute rest,
    Before I must ketch my ship–
For my watch was due in a minute or two,
    And I'd signed for the entire trip.

Now a shark, he ain't so bad as they paint,
    And a lobster's middlin' good,
And a clam or a shad, they ain't so bad,
    If properly understood.
But never rely on a sponge, says I,
    If you do, you'll be dam well done–
Even varmints and pests has hearts in their breasts,
    But a sponge, he ain't got none!

[* The orlop is a partial deck that "over laps" the bilge — RS]

He sponged the pay from my purse, that day,
  And he sponged my sweetheart's locket;
He sponged the quid from my cheek, he did,
  And the rum from my pistol pocket.
And he sponged my hair, till my head's as bare
  As you've noticed it is, no doubt,
He sponged me clean as a soup tureen—
  And then he kicked me out.

You kin trust in girls that hennas their curls,
  And men that powders their nose;
You kin trust in fakes and venomous snakes
  And dealers in second-hand clo'es.
A stealer of sheep sometimes will weep,
  And a loan-shark's bosom will smart
With Sym-path-ce, but on land or sea
  A Sponge ain't got no heart!

Ted Robinson, *Cleveland Plain Dealer*, November 26, 1924

A Landsman's Chantey

The restless sea is calling me,
    But I'm blessed if I will go,
I've sailed enough; the food was tough
    And the cruise was long and slow.
The skipper's mate was a hard-boiled skate,
    The bo's'n hard as nails,
We were long delayed at the ports we made,
    From bucking the howling gales.

The crew was scum, the berths were bum,
    And the engineer a fake,
And the steersman's game was to write his name
    In the bubbling, foaming wake.
So I guess I'll stay beside the bay
    Where the Tramps* pass, outward bound,
And the fog rolls in as thick as sin
    And the long green breakers pound.

And I'll watch them sail in the wintery gale,
    And burn my driftwood log
And smoke a pipe when the time is ripe
    And I'll drink my lonely grog,
But, the truth to tell, I'd like, like hell,
    To be cabin boy or cook
On the rustiest boat that can stay afloat,
    And be sailing for the Hook.

And I'd eat the slum, never mind how bum,
    And I'd swear again at the mate–
But I won't you know, I cannot go,
    I'm anchored in port by fate.

Bill Marlin, *Boston Herald*, January 14, 1929

[* Tramp Steamers, ships that pick up random cargo by chance or availability
without a specific schedule. Likewise, the crew is often hired without regard
to their skill and documentation (seaman's papers) -– RS]

The Sea

Yo ho! A chantey of the sea,
    Where tempests rage and flappers lave;
The salty deep, the mystery,
    About whose freedom statesmen rave.

It sets the lobster pots agog,
    It houses clams and soft shell crabs,
It is unpleasant in a fog,
    And slows seagoing taxicabs.

It turns the lubber sadly green
    And quite controls the appetite;
Initiated the marine,
    And looks majestically at night.

It is to blame for lots of things—
    Long Branch, Atlantic City, too;
It wears whitecaps and has its flings,
    And then again is truly blue.

It murmurs like a little child,
    Like maniac colossal yells;
Its floors are with Saharas piled;
    It certainly can shift the shells.

It is a favorite with whales;
    The herring loves it and the shark;
It runs to weeds and woeful gales;
    'Tis smooth and green as any park.

Yo ho! ye he! The heaving brine,
    The center of the world's unrest;
Some people say it is divine,
    While others like the mountains best.

Maurice Morris, *New York Herald*, August 18, 1922

Homeward Bound

Roud No. 927

To the Indian Ocean, we'll bid adieu;
    The Old Muscat and Zanzibar, too.
With her cargo stowed,
    The Cape we'll round.
With a song and cheer –
    For we're Homeward Bound

Chorus: Hurrah, we're homeward bound,
            Hurrah, hurrah, we're homeward bound;
        With a song and cheer –
        We're homeward bound.

And when we land on Providence dock
    The land sharks they will all begin to flock;
With a smirk and a smile,
    They will seem to say;
"You're welcome, Jack, with your twelve months pay."

Chorus: Hurrah, we're homeward bound,
            Hurrah, hurrah, we're homeward bound;
        With a song and cheer –
        We're homeward bound.

The above lines were those remembered of a sailor song composed by a young sailor named Randall, coming up Narragansett Bay on his return from a voyage around the world. This was probably composed 50 years ago and, to the writer's knowledge, has never been published. Thinking there might be descendants of Sailor Randall's who have retained a copy of this song. I appeal to you for assistance and shall greatly appreciate your kind efforts to this end.   F.H.S.

Sailor Randall, [Providence, Rhode Island] *Evening Bulletin,* March 23, 1916

The Dawn of a Better Cigarette

In days of old, when pirates bold
    Spread terror on the main,
They scuttled ships on pleasure trips,
    And had a bloody reign.

Their gleeful tunes of gold doubloons,
    Were sung in ev'ry port,
To go in quest of treasure chest
    Was their idea of sport.

Now seas are rid of Captain Kidd,
    And others of his set,
Yet men still seek, each bloody week,
    The Treasured Cigarette.

If you are smart you'll need no chart,
    To make a gladsome haul,
You'll find Old Gold, where are sold,
    The Treasure of Them All.

Advertisement in *Boston Herald*, June 25, 1926

A Shipping Clerk Chantey

Oh, a crate may go to Liverpool,
    Christina or Rangoon,
And a man may cross the Hudson
    On a Sunday afternoon.

I lay a stencil on dull, dead things,
    Give it an inky slap,
And the dull, dead things are hustled away
    To the further edge of the map.

To the further edge of the map some go;
    Others go not to far,
But all of them wander about in a sky
    Where I am a fast fixed star.

Thumb your Baedeker if you will,
    And talk of your year in Rome;
Yet I'm more of the world than the best of you:
    I never have lived at home!

No home but a world of names is mine,
    Stencils hung on the wall,
Teasing, beckoning words of brass...
    And I shall follow them all.

You who watch for me, four flights up,
    Women, waiting and wan,
These are names that you ought to fear:
    Lima, Singapore, Pran:

And if, some night when you wait for me,
    You should still be waiting at dawn,
Know that the stencils were stronger than you,
    Know that your lover has gone.

Oh, a crate may go to Liverpool,
    Christina or Rangoon,
And a man may cross the Hudson,
    On a Sunday afternoon.

Weare Holbrook, New York Press, November 30, 1919

Landlubber's Chantey

My Captain is far on the sea,
    And his eyes are upon a star,
And he follows his guiding star,
    And he smiles at the crystal star,
So what does he need of me?
    Yo-ho, Oh, what does he need of me?

My Captain is far on the sea,
    With his hands firm upon his wheel,
Misting sprays brush across his wheel,
    Caressing his hands on the wheel,
So what does he need of me?
    Yo-ho, Oh, what doe he need of me?

My Captain is far on the sea,
    And the waves give him music there,
And the waves give him comfort there,
    And the waves drown his sorrow there,
So what does he need of me?
    Yo-ho, Oh, what doe he need of me?

My Captain is far on the sea,
    And he knows that my home is his,
But he knows that the sea is his,
    That the sweet, cruel sea is his,
So what does he need of me?
    Yo-ho, Oh, what doe he need of me?

Helene Claiborne, [West Palm Beach] *Tampa Tribune*, December 9, 1928

A Land Chantey

I'd like to be a mariner,
    And sail the seven seas.
From Rio to Bering straits,
    Where casks of whiskey freeze.
I yearn to voyage here and there,
    To countries near and far.
From Labrador to Hawaii,
    From Nome to Zanzibar.

I'm crazy to go steaming down,
    Beneath a full white moon.
The muddy Irrawaddy
    To the temples of Rangoon.
Or flirt with dark-eyed houris
    Through a lattice in Algiers.
Or meet a priestly Tibetan
    Who has not bathed for years.

I'd hail with joy a rickshaw ride
    Along Calcutta's streets,
I'd climb the Alps where still no doubt
    The untamed nanny bleats.
In Hong Kong I would dearly love
    To drink a cup of tea.
The Bubbling Well Road has a most
    Romantic sound to me.

I dream about Pacific isles
    Of coral reefs and palms.
Or wallowing a lonely course,
    Beset by storms and calms.
But I am fated on the land
    Forever more to stay.
For I'm deadly seasick even when
    I go to Rockaway.

Minna Irving, *New York Herald*, August 25, 1921

Airplane Chantey

A letter from Avridge Mann with apologies to the *Round-the-World Flyers.*

Heave Ho! On the blades, my hearties!
    We're going to sail away!
We'll circle the globe, my hearties,
    The Aeronautical way!
And the engine sings as we flap our wings
    Like the wings of a duckling's daughter,
And away we go, as we sing, Yo, Ho!
    Yo, Ho! And a bottle of water!

We're up in the air, my hearties!
    And westward we turn our prow!
High flyers* are we, my hearties;
    The world is our oyster now!
And our ears we muff with a power puff,
    In a manner we hadn't oughter,
But away we go, as we sing, Yo, Ho!
    Yo, Ho! And a bottle of water!

We're flying around, my hearties!
    Around the terrestrial sphere!
We're stopping at towns, my hearties,
    Whose names you will seldom hear!
With our many stops we are full of hops,
    Like the Rock ere the Volstead caught 'er,
So away we go, as we sing, Yo, Ho!
    Yo, Ho! And a bottle of water!

Avridge Mann, *Seattle Star,* April 2, 1924

Old Man of the Sea

As the World Wags: Speaking of Betty Martin, my grandmother sung this about her:

> Hi Betty Martin, tip-toe fine;
> If you want a husband, you can't have mine.

Betty's possible want of a soul mate seems to have worried the general public considerably at one time. I wonder if anyone knows the queer song our nurse used to sing to us; I am sure she made many mistakes and mispronounced many words, for she did in all the rest of the songs she sang to us. It was, as nearly as I can remember it, like this:

> There was an old man came over the sea
> Who my heart or naught I had him
> Came over the sea a wooing me
> Winsome, ransom, glorious, handsome
> Filly ma dink ma da.

> My father told me to set him a stool;
> Who my heart or naught I had him
> I set him a stool and he sat like a fool.
> Winsome, ransom, glorious, handsome
> Filly ma dink ma da.

> My father told me to light him to bed,
> Who my heart or naught I had him
> I lit him to bed and he asked me to wed.
> Winsome, ransom, glorious, handsome
> Filly ma dink ma da.

> My father to me to go to the church,
> Who my heart or naught I had him
> I went to the church with a pocket full of birch.
> Winsome, ransom, glorious, handsome
> Filly ma dink ma da.

I laid the birch up on the shelf,
  Who my heart or naught I had him
If you want any more you can sing it yourself.
  Winsome, ransom, glorious, handsome
    Filly ma dink ma da.

The doggerel refrain appeared, of course, in every verse, the last two lines being sung as fast as possible. It seems as if the second line might originally have made sense. I always was curious about the significance of birch in the pocket at a wedding. Whether it was bark or leaves. I fancied it was of some value as it was "laid on the shelf" carefully after the bride's return home.

We all sang it with much gusto when young but I hadn't thought of it for years.

E.L.A., Boston Herald, Saturday August 25, 1923

Quaint Sea Chantey
or **Further Thoughts on New England Accents**
By a Mystified Westerner

In Lynn, in Swampscott and Nahant
  Many an extra consonant.

Nestles in the native speech,
  Numerous as pebbles on the beach.

Plenteous as sands upon the shore
  Are those who like their oysters "rawr"!

To Captain William James McCommer
  His legal spouse is known as "Mommer";

Yet Captain Bill's seafaring "bruthah"
  Will designate his wife as "Mothah".

Where "r's" should be they often aren't...
  Can you tell why? I know I carn't.

Henrietta Fort Holland, Boston Herald, August 27, 1934

The Sailor's Landlady

Tune: *Knight of the Raven Black Plume*

A landlady at the bar with her glasses,
    Her tapster stood silently by,
Says, look out Tom and see who there passes,
    If a sailor, pray bid him draw nigh –

Chorus: Landlady, landlady, banish thy gloom,
        For here is a sailor with shiners come home.
        Landlady, landlady, banish thy gloom,
        For here is a sailor with shiners come home.

The landlady arose from her seat,
    And through the green curtain she spied
A sailor returned in the fleet,
    That was riding at anchor outside –

Then soon in the front of the door,
    She curtsied quite down to the sill,
Saying you're welcome brave Jack now on shore,
    Walk in, call and drink what you will –

Chorus: Sailor boy, Sailor boy, banish thy gloom,
        Your landlady's glad to see you safe home.
        Sailor boy, Sailor boy, banish thy gloom,
        Your landlady's glad to see you safe home.

I have lately crossed over the sea,
    I came from a far distant strand –
My two years hard earnings, I have with me,
    So landlady give us your hand;

And here is my purse, you may take it,
    'Tis safer with you than with me;
And here is my watch 'lest I should break it,
    I willingly give it to thee, –

Chorus: Sailor boy, Sailor boy, banish thy gloom,
           Your landlady's glad to see you safe home.
       Sailor boy, Sailor boy, banish thy gloom,
           Your landlady's glad to see you safe home.

The landlady then filled up her glass,
   And the bar room with revelry rang,
While Jack by the side of his lass,
   Half seas over, in joyous notes sang,

Chorus: Landlady, Landlady, banish thy gloom,
           I have money to spend, and for that I came home.
       Landlady, Landlady, banish thy gloom,
           I have money to spend, and for that I came home.

The sailor awoke in the morning,
   And found himself out in the street,
His head with a fever was burning,
   And the storm raged, with rain and with sleet –

Chorus: Landlady, landlady, open the door,
           'Tis Jack thy old friend, let me in I implore.
       Landlady, landlady, open the door,
           'Tis Jack thy old friend, let me in I implore.

The landlady opened her curtain,
   Go off you imposter, she said,
I ne'er saw your face I am certain,
   Don't disturb honest folks in their bed –

Chorus: Sailor dog, sailor dog, away from my door,
           I can't let you in, I ne'er saw you before.
       Sailor dog, sailor dog, away from my door,
           I can't let you in, I ne'er saw you before.

by A Tar, *Alexander Gazette,* September 9, 1837

The Hero in the Stroke-Hole

While you sing of Schley and Hobson,
    And the gallant Dewey, too.
While with thoughts of them your hearts are all aglow.
    I would sing you another –
Just as brave and just as true –
    Of the man who does the stoking down below.

For his home is in the hell,
    Down below,
And he doesn't hear the yell,
    Down below,
That goes up when firing's done,
When the ship he's with has won –
He must keep a-shoveling on,
    Down below.

Though his name be never mentioned,
    Though we see or know him not,
Though his deeds may never bring him worldly fame.
    He's a man above the others –
And the bravest of the lot
    And the hero of the battle just the same.

He's the man who does the work,
    Down below,
From the labor does not shirk,
    Down below, –
He is shoveling day and night,
Feeding flames a-blazing bright,
Keeping up a killing fire,
    Down below.

In the awful heat and torture
 Of the fires that leap and dance
In and out the furnace doors that never close,
 On in silence he must work.
For with him there's ne'er a chance
 On his brow to feel the outer breeze that blows.

For they've locked him in a room,
 Down below,
In a burning, blazing tomb,
 Down below,
Where he cannot see the sky,
Cannot learn in time to fly,
When destruction stalketh nigh,
 Down below.

While the fighting fierce is waging,
 And the cannon overhead
With their sizzling shells the enemy surround,
 To the stoker down below,
Not a word is ever said,
 To his ear is borne no echo of the sound.

When they open wide the door,
 Down below.
And they cry, "Your work is o'er,
 Down below!"
There they find him weakly lying
On a pile of coal and crying,
Out in madness, for he's dying
 Down below.

San Antonio Light, July 15, 1898

Acknowledgments

I extend my gratitude to Jennifer, my wife, for her continued support and research work at the Salem Public Library. I would also like to thank shantyman Gary Foreman, retired USS Constitution Museum, Manager of Visitor Services and Interpretation, Steve Woodbury, for his editorial suggestions and proofreading, Peter and Audi Souza, leaders of the local chantey group, *Three Sheets to the Wind*, and marine photographer Mary Barker. Thanks to the following libraries and online archives for their resources: *Salem Links and Lore* at the Salem Public Library, *Roud Index* at the Vaughan Williams Memorial Library, Boston Public Library, Library of Congress, Phillips Library, Newpapers.com, Ancestry.com, and GenealgyBank.com.

Lastly, I would like to acknowledge all our music friends and local sessions for which we all share our love of music and community.

Enjoy and keep on singing.

Bob Strom

Nautical photographer Mary Barker is the photographer and social media manager for the *Gloucester Marine Railways* and is the official photographer for the *Schooner Adventure*. Mary has a candid, documentary style of photography focusing on existing light and minimal editing to affect a natural, realistic photographic outcome. Mary strives to capture the essence of historic boat restoration and commercial operations.

Mary continues to publish her photographs in several national magazines, including *Wooden Boat*, *Marlinspike*, the *National Maritime Historical Society*, local newspapers, brochures, and many travel magazines. Bob Strom features several of her photographs in the two-volume music collection *Old Salem in Ballad* and *Song* and *Old Salem at Sea in Ballad and Song*.

Mary continues to expand her passion from documenting wooden ship restorations on the *Schooners Adventure, Roseway, Ernestina, the Mayflower, Phyllis A,* and *Formidable* to photographing commercial fishing vessels and their operations.

Bibliography

"A Whaling We'll All Go," *Nantucket Inquirer*, January 6, 1827, pg. 2.

Acree, Mrs. Sharlie F., "Who Go Down to the Sea in Ships,"
Houston Post, April 4, 1926, pg. 78.

Allison, Young E., "The Dead Men's Song," *Harrisburg* [Pennsylvania]
Patriot, May 29, 1919, pg. 10.

"Billi Bumper," *Hartford Times*, February 15, 1820, pg. 2.

"Blow a Man Down," *New Orleans Item*, June 9, 1918, pg. 9.

"Blow the Man Down," *New Orleans States*, December 8, 1929, pg. 42.

Braley, Berton, "Deep Sea Chantey," *San Antonio Light*,
February 23, 1923, pg. 6.

Brotherton, Alice Williams, "The Gulf Chantey," *New York Times*, re
printed in *Baltimore American*, August 14, 1917, pg. 6.

Bryant, Esq., W.C., "Corn-Shucking Song," *New York Evening Post*,
and *Salem Register*, May 1, 1843, pg. 1.

Bungan, Paul, "Sea Chantey," *Seattle Daily Times*, August 12, 1927, pg. 6.

"Canaday I.O.," *Sunday Times*, [Michigan] *Bay City Times*,
January 19, 1902, pg. 12.

"Capstan Chantey, A," *New York Daily Tribune*, December 12, 1913, pg. 9.

Carcass, "A Chantey of Wild Wives," *Chicago Daily News*,
July 22, 1922, pg. 4.

"Chain Gang Chantey," *Cleveland Plain Dealer*, January 20, 1935, pg. 12.

"Chantey Bill," *San Diego Union*, June 6, 1926, pg. 88.

"Chantey of Cap'n Foster, The," *Boston Herald*, January 20, 1924, pg. 36.

"Chantey of the River," *Omaha Monitor*, June 18, 1926, pg. 5.

Claiborne, Helene, "Landlubber's Chantey," [West Palm Beach]
Tampa Tribune, December 9, 1928, pg. 38.

Collins, Dean. "Canine Chantey," *Portland Oregonian*,
November 21, 1914, pg. 6.

D'Argyle, Duc, "The Dry Chief's Chantey," *Trenton Evening Times*,
July 5, 1922, pg. 1.

"Dawn of a Better Cigarette, The," *Boston Herald*, June 25, 1926, pg. 11.

"Derby (Darby) Ram, The," *Boston Christian Register*, May 13, 1876, pg. 4.

Dix—n, R.M., "Forecastle Rhymery," *Nantucket Inquirer*,
March 26, 1836, pg. 1.

"Dover Chantey," *Rock Island Argus and Daily Union*,
    December 1, 1921, pg. 7.

"Dry Navy Chantey," *Trenton Evening Times,* July 7, 1922, pg. 1.

"Dutchman, The," *New Orleans Item*, June 9, 1918, pg. 15.

"Fair Betty," *Daily Illinois State Journal*, August 13, 1922, pg. 28.

"Grog Tune," *Boston Herald*, March 25, 1918, pg. 10.

Guest, Edgar. "The Gulf of Mexico," *Houston Chronicle*,
    October 12, 1933, pg. 16.

"Haul Away Rosy," *Christian Science Monitor*, reprinted in *Iowa Evening
    Nonpareil,* June 17, 1920, pg. 12.

Henry, "A Wall Street Chantey," *Springfield*, [Massachusetts] *Republican*,
    May 28, 1933, pg. 12.

"Hero in the Stroke-Hole, The," *San Antonio Light,* July 15, 1898, pg. 6.

Holbrook, Weare, "A Shipping Clerk Chantey," *New York Press*,
    November 30, 1919, pg. 73.

Holland, Henrietta Fort, "Quaint Sea Chantey," *Boston Herald*,
    August 27, 1934, pg. 10.

Ireland, Baron, "Cap'n Sears Kendrick," *New York Herald*,
    November 11, 1922, pg. 108.

Ireland, Baron, "Egbert Phillips," *New York Herald*,
    November 26, 1922, pg. 108.

Ireland, Baron, "Judah Cahoon," *New York Herald*,
    November 28, 1922, pg. 108.

Ireland, Baron, "Tongues A-waggin'," *New York Herald*,
    November 28, 1922, pg. 108.

Irving, Minna, "A Land Chantey," *Maryland Gazette*,
    August 25, 1921, pg. 6.

"Jimmy Yole's Chantey," *Boston Herald,* January 19, 1926, pg. 1.

"John Brown's Body," *Washington D.C., Evening Star,*
    August 8, 1924, pg. 65.

Knights, Clifford Reynolds, "Your Song," *Trenton Evening Times,*
    May 9, 1920, pg. 3.

"Learn About Drinking From Me," *Greensboro* [North Carolina] *Record,*
    September 17, 1928, pg. 5.

"Life on the Ocean Wave, A," *Oregonian*, December 12, 1916, pg. 11.

"Long Chantey, The," *New Orleans Item,* June 9, 1918, pg. 9.

Levy, Newman, "A Deep Sea Chantey," *New York Daily Tribune,*
    November 8, 1919, pg. 17.

Mackley, J.H., "Sailor Song," *The Cleveland Plain Dealer,*
  October 3, 1894, pg. 4.

Mann, Avridge, "Airplane Chantey," *Seattle Star,* April 2, 1924, pg. 7.

Marlin, Bill, "A Landsman's Chantey," *Boston Herald,*
  January 14, 1929, pg. 10.

Mathias, T.H., "The Homeward Bound," *The San Francisco Seamen's
  Journal,* and *Cleveland Plain Dealer,* June 11, 1899, pg. 28.

McColl, John, "An Amateur Chantey," *New Orleans Item,*
  September 27, 1918, pg. 4.

Montague, James J., "The Uplift Sea," *Springfield* [Massachusetts]
  Republican, August 30, 1934, pg. 10.

Morris, Maurice, "The Sea," New York Herald, August 18, 1922, pg. 9.

M.T.C., "To the Heart of the Dead, Dead Calm," [Philadelphia] *Evening
  Public Ledger,* July 17, 1920, pg. 7.

"Natchez, The," *Harrisburg Patriot,* March 6, 1875, pg. 3.

"Off to Sea Once More," *San Antonio Light,* January 26, 1919, pg. 11.

"Oh! The Gertrude Steer!," *New York Daily Post,* October 22, 1863, pg. 2.

"Old Man of the Sea," *Boston Herald,* Saturday August 25, 1923, pg. 10.

"Our Own Bootlegger Chantey," *Springfield* [Massachusetts] *Daily News,*
  October 21, 1922, pg. 4.

"Oyster Time Chantey," *Richmond Times Dispatch,*
  September 3, 1916, pg. 12.

"Paddy' Noisiest and Best," *San Antonio Light,* January 28, 1919, pg. 11.

Patterson, J.E., "Banks of the Sacramento," *New York Daily Tribune,*
  September 9, 1900, pg. 9.

Parker, Dorothy, "Chantey," [Michigan] *Adrian,* May 4, 1925, pg. 4.

Phillips, H.I., "The Telephonic Sea Chanties," *New Orleans Item,*
  December 19, 1929, pg. 20.

"Phoenix House," *New Orleans Item,* June 9, 1918, pg. 15.

Powers, M.J., "The Great Lake Chantey," *New Orleans Item,*
  June 9, 1918, pg. 9.

Powers, M.J., "The Pier Head Chantey," *New Orleans Item,*
  June 9, 1918, pg. 9.

"Pull Down Below," *New Orleans Item,* June 9, 1918, pg. 9.

R.M.P. Jr., "Billy Bone's Fancy," [Philadelphia] *Evening Public Ledger,*
  December 27, 1920, pg. 14.

Reedy, W. Curran, "Down Lima Way," *Birmingham Herald,*
  July 11, 1919, pg. 5.

"Riverside Drive Chantey, A," *New York Daily,* October 20, 1920, pg. 9.

Robinson, Henry Morton, "Chantey of Notorious Bibbers," reprinted from the F.P.A.'s "Coming Tower," *New York World, Boston Herald,* July 1, 1927, pg. 53.

Robinson, Ted, "A Dipsea Chantey," *Cleveland Plain Dealer,* November 26, 1924, pg. 8.

Roberts, Theodore, "Fiddler's Green," *Springfield* [Massachusetts] *Republic,* July 26, 1903, pg. 17.

"Row Well Ye Mariners," *English Melodies from the 13th to the 18th Centuries,* J.M. Dent & Sons, *Quincy Patriot Ledger,* December 20, 1928, pg. 7.

"Rum Chasers' Chantey," *Trenton Evening Times,* May 8, 1925, pg. 1.

"Sailor's Chantey, A," *Colorado Springs Gazette,* September 9, 1918, pg. 4.

"Sailor's Landlady, The," *Alexander Gazette,* September 9, 1837, pg. 3.

Sailor Randall, "Homeward Bound," [Providence, Rhode Island] *Evening Bulletin,* March 23, 1916, pg. 23.

"Sally In Our Alley," *New Orleans Item,* June 9, 1918, pg. 15.

Sargent, Ray, "A Longshoreman Chantey," *N.Y. Tribune,* reprinted in the *Evening Journal,* October 30, 1919, pg. 5.

"Screwmen, The," *New Orleans Item,* September 9, 1918, pg. 9.

Sheekman, Arthur "High Water Chantey," *Chicago Daily Times,* September 19, 1929, pg. 14.

"Shenandoah," *New York Tribune,* March 4, 1893, pg. 5.

Shields, Art, "A Roving Wrecker's Chantey," *New York Daily Worker,* May 7, 1927, pg. 5.

Smiles, Billy, "The Dreadnought's Song," *Sun and New York Press,* May 30, 1917, pg. 13.

"Song of Captain Kidd, The," [Chicago] *Daily Inner Ocean,* November 29, 1879, pg. 4.

"South Australia," *Boston Journal,* March 29, 1903, pg. 5.

"Sponger Money or The Key West Chantey," *Key West Citizen,* December 31, 1945, pg. 6.

Stone, Harold Otho, "The Klondike Cow, A Chantey of the North," *Anchorage Daily Times,* May 10, 1923, pg. 6.

"Susan Peters, The," *Pawtucket Times,* September 9, 1906, pg. 13.

"Sweep Over a Sailor's Grave," The Seamen's Widow and Orphan Association, *Salem Register,* February 9, 1854, pg. 2.

Swift, Otis Peabody, "Leave Her, Johnny, Leave Her," Press Publishing Company, *San Antonio Light,* January 26, 1919, pg. 11.

Thomas, Rowland, "An Off Shore Chantey," *American Magazine*,
   reprinted in *Omaha World Herald*, March 11, 1910, pg. 2.
Thornton, Arthur, "Liverpool Rope," *New York Press*,
   March 23, 1919, pg. 29.
"Tip From the Cook in the Galley, A," *Seattle Daily Times*,
   June 23, 1918, pg. 25.
"We're the Crew of Pierre Le Rouge," *Knoxville News*, April 6, 1934, pg. 9
"Whaler's Chantey," The King of the Black Isles, *Boston Herald*,
   April 7, 1923, pg. 8.
"What Pleases The Girls," Found by Beth and Jeff Welin,
   Manchester Historical Society, *Salem Gazette*, mid 1850s.
Wilder, Chief Sea Scout James A., "The Sea Scout's Chantey,"
   Judsonia [Arkansas] *Weekly*, October 16, 1919, pg. 3.
"Windlass Song," *Salem Register*, October 24, 1853, pg. 1.
Yankee Blade, "Goin' Fishin'," *Canton* [Ohio] *Repository*,
   February 2, 1893, pg. 8.

Web Resources

Ancestry
   www.Ancestry.com
Boston Public Library
   www.bpl.org
Commonwealth Catalog
   www.noblenet.org/comcat/
EBSCO
   www.ebsco.com/
Genealogy Bank
   www.genealogybank.com
Library of Congress
   www.loc.gov

Historical Newspapers
   www.Newspapers.com
Mary Barker
   www.mabarkerphoto.com
Phillips Library
   www.pem.org/visit/library
Salem Athenaeum
   www.salemathenaeum.net
Salem Public Library
   www.salempl.org
Salem Links and Lore
   www.noblenet.org